own your life

*Living with deep intention, bold faith,
and generous love*

SALLY CLARKSON

**TYNDALE®
MOMENTUM**

*An Imprint of
Tyndale House Publishers*

D0967609

Visit Tyndale online at www.tyndale.com.

Visit Tyndale Momentum online at www.tyndalemomentum.com.

Visit Sally Clarkson at www.SallyClarkson.com.

TYNDALE, Tyndale Momentum, and the Tyndale Momentum logo are registered trademarks of Tyndale House Publishers, Inc. Tyndale Momentum is an imprint of Tyndale House Publishers, Inc.

Own Your Life: Living with Deep Intention, Bold Faith, and Generous Love

Copyright © 2014 by Sally Clarkson. All rights reserved.

Some content first appeared at www.itakejoy.com.

Cover photograph of flower copyright © Alan Shapiro/Stocksy. All rights reserved.

Cover texture copyright © pondkungz/Shutterstock. All rights reserved.

Designed by Jennifer Phelps

Unless otherwise indicated, all Scripture quotations are taken from the New American Standard Bible,® copyright © 1960, 1962, 1963, 1968, 1971, 1972, 1973, 1975, 1977, 1995 by The Lockman Foundation. Used by permission.

Scripture quotations marked NLT are taken from the *Holy Bible*, New Living Translation, copyright © 1996, 2004, 2007, 2013 by Tyndale House Foundation. Used by permission of Tyndale House Publishers, Inc., Carol Stream, Illinois 60188. All rights reserved.

Scripture quotations marked ESV are taken from *The Holy Bible*, English Standard Version® (ESV®), copyright © 2001 by Crossway, a publishing ministry of Good News Publishers. Used by permission. All rights reserved.

Scripture quotations marked NIV are taken from the Holy Bible, *New International Version*,® NIV.® Copyright © 1973, 1978, 1984, 2011 by Biblica, Inc.® (Some quotations may be from the earlier NIV edition, copyright © 1984.) Used by permission. All rights reserved worldwide.

Scripture quotations marked HCSB are taken from the Holman Christian Standard Bible,® copyright © 1999, 2000, 2002, 2003, 2009 by Holman Bible Publishers. Used by permission. Holman Christian Standard Bible,® Holman CSB,® and HCSB® are federally registered trademarks of Holman Bible Publishers.

Library of Congress Cataloging-in-Publication Data

Clarkson, Sally.
  Own your life : living with deep intention, bold faith, and generous love / Sally Clarkson.
    pages cm
  Includes bibliographical references.
  ISBN 978-1-4143-9128-1 (sc)
1. Christian life. 2. Christian women—Religious life. I. Title.
  BV4501.3.C527 2014
  248.4—dc23   2014036432

Printed in the United States of America

20	19	18	17	16	15
7	6	5	4	3	2

APR 0 1 2015

JUN X X 2015

If you've ever wondered what a life well lived looks like, you'll find the secret between the pages of this book. Sally Clarkson generously opens up her story with the hospitality of a mentor, a mother, and a friend wrapped into one. On these pages you'll discover inspiring examples of what life to the full can look like when you are fully surrendered to Christ.

LISA-JO BAKER
Author of *Surprised by Motherhood* and community manager for (in)courage

Since the time my children were babies, I have been so challenged by reading Sally Clarkson's writings. She's inspired me to embrace each day, find simple ways to cultivate beauty in my home, and take time to invest in myself so that I can better nurture and bless my family. If you are a busy woman who longs to live with meaning and purpose, you'll be blessed by reading *Own Your Life*. It's packed with heartfelt encouragement and practical strategies to help you savor life more and make each moment count.

CRYSTAL PAINE
New York Times bestselling author of *Say Goodbye to Survival Mode* and founder of MoneySavingMom.com

Sally is a woman teeming with wisdom and zest for life, and they're contagious both in her presence and in her written words. Every moment I've shared with her has been a blessing, and it's an honor for all of us that she so graciously shares her life lessons and timeless truths in her writing.

TSH OXENREIDER
Author of *Notes from a Blue Bike*

Life was made to be lived with purpose. But sometimes our busy and broken lives get in the way of our intentions. *Own Your Life* is more than an inspirational book; it's a guidebook to living a life that matters.

KRISTEN WELCH
Author of *Rhinestone Jesus*; http://wearethatfamily.com

Sally writes with as much compassion and concern as she displays when chatting with a dear friend. She and her husband have an abundance of experience, including thirty years of marriage, parenting, world travel, and more, and the interesting personal stories Sally shares provide solid,

WITHDRAWN

incredibly applicable wisdom. As she intimately draws you into each story, her words will break down the barriers that keep you from owning your life and will motivate you to fulfill your God-given purpose.

JENNIFER SMITH
Author of *The Unveiled Wife* and founder of Unveiledwife.com

Too often we get caught up in the daily chaos, and we miss the realization that we're leaving a legacy. *Own Your Life* shows readers how to live the God-shaped destiny designed for them. Living for God's Kingdom and glory is something Sally Clarkson does with all that she is . . . and now her caring, wise voice guides readers on how to do the same. This book is perfect to read with a friend or small group. Highly recommended!

TRICIA GOYER
Author of forty-five books, including *Balanced*

This book, rich with the wisdom of a life lived intentionally, is a gift to women of all ages. It's the tool we need to ask God what He wants us to dream for Him and how He wants us to live that dream. Sally emboldens and equips us to make faith-filled choices and to live with generous love, no matter what the cost. She meets us where we are— in the hard places of real life—and gently leads us to where God waits to mold us into our best selves.

ELIZABETH FOSS
Author of *Real Learning* and coauthor of *Small Steps for Catholic Moms*; www.elizabethfoss.com

Sally Clarkson has always been such an incredible inspiration to me as I've fumbled along this path of parenting, and I count myself blessed to have her words and wisdom mentor me along the way. Once again, Sally has written a book full of godly advice and wisdom, pointing us to the ultimate example and mentor of all. As I read *Own Your Life*, I found myself feeling as though I was cozied up on Sally's couch with a warm cup of tea, soaking up every bit of motherly and yet godly wisdom on how to truly live a beautiful life of balance and purpose.

SUMMER SALDANA
Writer/blogger at SummerSaldana.com

COMING HOME TO GOD: FINDING YOUR PART IN HIS STORY

God is our refuge and strength,
A very present help in trouble.
Therefore we will not fear, though the earth should change
And though the mountains slip into the heart of the sea.
PSALM 46:1-2

"Mama, the world seems like a very scary place, and it makes me feel powerless. I am afraid I will be so lonely and insecure without friends and family around me."

Joy, my daughter, would be leaving the next day to study in Oxford, England, and we had just finished zipping her last suitcase shut. She had been looking forward to her semester abroad as a great adventure and inspiring opportunity. Yet as we were packing that day, a second American journalist had been beheaded by ISIS (Islamic State of Iraq and Syria). The media was also talking about terrorist threats to England and the United States. Between that news and the devastating reports of earthquakes, war, and immorality among Christian leaders, Joy was understandably feeling overwhelmed. Of course, as a mom, those same thoughts and fears had run through my mind.

"Can we have one last time together out on the grass, under the stars?" she pleaded. "I need some peace before I go to bed." She knew that it was late and that we were both exhausted after getting all the details in place for her flight and for spending three months away from home.

"Yes, my sweet precious," I whispered, calling her by the special nickname I use whenever we have heart-to-heart talks. "We will make one more memory together!"

As was our habit, we took some soft, old blankets out to our front yard and lay next to each other under the tall pines, shoulder to shoulder on the grass. A dog barked and the cold mountain air blew gently across the aspen leaves in the distance, but otherwise, the night was clear and quiet. Silently sharing the moment, we gazed up. Stars filled the navy-blue sky and sparkled as though just for us. We breathed out the life clutter of the day and inhaled the peacefulness of the grandeur above us.

"Mama, when I look at what God has done and *keep my eyes on Him,* my fears seem to melt away," Joy whispered as she snuggled closer.

Our family, which includes five authors, is truly philosophical, a people of words. God's voice seemed to be speaking through my own heart as well. In our last moments together, I wanted to lift Joy up to Him, to leave her with courage, and to assure her of the One who would care for her.

"Joy, this vast display of stars and all the galaxies beyond have been held in place by the sure, strong hands of God for thousands of years—through wars, tragedies, and disasters of every kind. Not one year of our history has shaken the power or control of God.

"Our God, who created this beauty for us to behold and who has shown His power through the calm night skies, wants to fill you from the tip of your toes to the top of your head with the very same energy that created all of this—the Spirit who threw the night sky into place—so that you will know His full companionship, love, beauty, and wisdom each step in your journey ahead.

"God has prepared a story for you to live. There will be many in Oxford who will long to know His love, something perhaps only you can show them. Others, looking for meaning, will need the messages of His truth that are stored in your soul. Those you meet who are filled with fear and despair will need your hope and faith. Teachers will be there to sharpen your mind so you can become a more excellent message maker. Beauty will be strewn across your path so you can observe His fingerprints. I know that if you embrace the days ahead, no matter what they hold, your time in Oxford will be significant and purposeful. You are a chosen one, and I know wherever you go you will bring His light and love.

"My sweet precious, you will always have a choice to make. If you look at the darkness and fear, you will grow dark in your soul. But if you look to God and trust Him with your days, you will reflect His reality in all of your words, your relationships, your work, and your celebrations. Don't look at the fear; just keep the memory of this night and His power and beauty always before your eyes and ever in your thoughts. And of course you know that you will be in my heart and in my prayers constantly."

If you, like Joy, sometimes feel fearful, alone, lost, or overwhelmed, my desire is that this book will encourage you to own your life and to live out your part of His story. I share the truths I have learned by walking hand in hand with God for many years.

I dedicate this book to my precious children—Sarah, Joel, Nathan, and Joy—and to all who need to know that they are not invisible to God. I want you to know that He loves you and is at work in your life, that He has designed your days and moments to be filled with significance, and that He has created you to tell a story. May He bless and strengthen your hearts and faith as you read the pages ahead.

CONTENTS

FOREWORD

by Sarah Mae, Angela Perritt, and Ruth Schwenk

My life journey has been scattered with so many heartfelt friends who feel like a kiss from God. Here, three such friends share what the concept of "own your life" has meant to them. Over the past five years, I have been hosting leadership training weekends in my home to personally focus on the hearts and spiritual lives of women. After attending one of the intensives, Sarah, Ruth, and Angela told me how transformed their lives have been by the content that began as a conference in my home and has now become this book.

During our time together I answered some of their questions: What has God called me to do? How do I raise kids to love God and others well? What difference can I make in this world? As a woman a couple of decades ahead of them in life, I enjoyed passing along some of the hard-won lessons I've learned; in turn, they have taught me much about living with wisdom, honesty, and grace.

After you've heard from them, I want to invite you into our conversation. My prayer is that, after you finish this book, you too will experience the meaning and satisfaction that come when you own your life.

–Sally

It was July.

Sally and I had just finished a lovely breakfast at the Broadmoor, a beautiful and ornate hotel in Colorado Springs. She had brought me there to spoil me and make me feel special; Sally has that way about her, wanting others to feel loved and valued.

After feasting on the fluffy eggs, crisp bacon, freshly squeezed orange juice, and more delicious offerings, Sally led me to a small, quiet space tucked away in a corner of the grand hotel. The little room, boasting a fireplace, couch, and two comfy chairs, beckoned us to sit awhile, and of course we did.

We filled up two hours in that place going through Scriptures and drinking tea as I poured my heart out for Sally to tend to. And she did. She tended to my heart and my soul, and when we left, I not only had received renewed vision for my life but also had stored away a game-changing phrase that has been at the forefront of most of my decisions since. The phrase was this: *Own your life.*

Sally taught me that a wise woman—that a wise *person*—takes responsibility for her choices and understands that "each person has the power and authority to bring his or her life back into order. Each of us is a steward of the days allotted for our lifetime."

Friends, Sally has done the work; she is a woman who has walked faithfully and with integrity throughout the seasons of her life, and she has words that are worth heeding.

Her gracious admonishment to own our lives and leave a legacy that matters is not just a sweet encouragement but also a life-changing call to live for God with all of who we are and in all the choices we make. And furthermore, Sally doesn't just tell us to own our lives; she tells us *how* we can do that.

I'm first in line for this message, and I'll be last in line as well, because I *need* these words. In fact, we all do. Our lives matter because God has a story for us to live for His Kingdom.

And to live it, we must be willing to own our lives.

—*Sarah Mae*
Coauthor of *Desperate: Hope for the Mom Who Needs to Breathe*

The fact of the matter is we all have but one life. Our time here is short—like a vapor, really. Here one day and gone the next. From the moment we take our first breaths, our days are numbered, so how we live matters. The decisions we make—the important ones and, yes, the mundane ones too—they all matter. Everyday decisions add up to form the life we live and the legacy we leave behind.

In *Own Your Life*, Sally Clarkson calls us to a stewardship of the precious life God has given us. It's important to keep the end goal—the legacy we leave behind—in mind because it helps us to be wise and discerning with our present-day decisions. I love the insights and challenges Sally gives to all of us, encouraging us to own our lives and explaining the importance of this intentional decision. Don't just sit back and let life happen to you: Engage it, embrace it, and live it out with intention, purpose, and trust in our Lord. Live a life of faith; don't be afraid to take risks and love those God has placed in your life.

Years from now, people may not remember your name, but the way you owned your life, the choices you made, the way you loved . . . your legacy . . . that is what will ripple through the generations who follow after you.

We may be here for just a moment, but let's make that moment really count! Honor God with the life He has given you by being wise in how you live . . . how you own your life.

—*Angela Perritt*
Coauthor of *You Are Loved*

I still remember the night I first met Sally Clarkson. Okay, I'll admit it—I was a bit starstruck! For years I had known Sally through her writings, so to get a chance to meet her in person was quite an honor. I had no idea that this night would be the beginning of a beautiful friendship that would challenge and inspire me as a wife, mom, speaker, blogger, and leader.

For the past three summers, I have had the privilege of spending time with Sally in her home and experiencing firsthand the message that burns so deeply within her: "Own your life." With wisdom, encouragement, and vision, she helped me see what I needed to change, what I needed to let go of, and what I needed to grab hold of in God's calling on my life.

Like you, I wear many hats. As a mom to four beautiful children, a pastor's wife, a speaker, a writer, and a blogger, it is difficult to imagine navigating this journey without Sally's friendship and insight. I am grateful that God has gifted me and other women in my generation with Sally's voice. Her message is one we desperately need. I am grateful to call her friend, mentor, and fellow chaser of dreams!

–*Ruth Schwenk*
Author of *The Better Mom* blog

THE BEGINNING

What Will Be the Legacy of Your Life?

"What will be the legacy of your life? What story will the days of your life tell? Will you invest your life for eternity, or spend it, wasting the days on things that do not matter, on issues that will quickly fade away?"

All eyes were glued on our earnest, solemn speaker, and a profound hush hovered over the packed gymnasium as we allowed his words to wrap themselves around our deepest thoughts.

More than seven thousand people had gathered for a national ministry's staff training conference at Colorado State University in 1976. The tension in the air was so heavy that it was almost palpable.

I was twenty-two and had just completed my first year in campus ministry at the University of Texas. My heart was filled with passion and excitement after being involved in personal ministry with hundreds of college students that year. I felt in awe at being part of a conference with so many seasoned staff members.

Although it was an annual conference, this year was different. The day before, about thirty-five of our women staff leaders had met for training at a retreat center in the nearby mountains. The weather that morning had been pleasant, but heavy downpours led to horrific flash flooding by evening. As the women relaxed together at the end of the day, they were startled by orders coming through bullhorns outside: "Evacuate immediately! A flood is coming this way! You must get into your cars and head for higher ground!"

The women raced to the cars and piled in, and they ended up driving in different directions. In the course of the raging flood, seven of our young staff women drowned in the surging waters. The sudden death of seven of our most vibrant leaders, who had lived passionately for Christ, reminded all of us in that gym of the preciousness and brevity of life and filled us with overwhelming grief.

Consequently, the words of the speaker, delivered just one day after the flood and the news of their deaths, flew like an arrow into my heart. At that moment, life seemed fragile, short, something to be honored and invested in with great intention and care. The speaker's words helped shape the destiny of my life by making me pay attention to the choices and decisions I was making at an early age.

Later that morning, another speaker shared passionately about how millions of people all over the world did not own a Bible or know the personal love of God. At the end of his talk, he announced an unprecedented opportunity for a team of missionaries to enter Communist Poland as teachers to bring the gospel to this suppressed country.

"If you have only one life to live, wouldn't you want the privilege of being strategic for the Kingdom of God?" he asked. "Will some of you consider joining us to bring the light of the gospel to this place?"

I sat riveted, my heart pounding, thinking, *Oh, how I wish I could have an opportunity to make a difference in this world! God, I am just a young, untrained, unskilled person, but I want You to use me during my lifetime. Please let them pick me to go if it is Your will. I am Your girl, forever.*

As soon as the meeting was over, I practically ran all the way to the international office. I wanted to be sure I was one of the first to fill out an application to be a part of the team to Poland. I knew they would probably not take me because I was so inexperienced, but I prayed all the way there. When I arrived, I was shocked to learn that only a handful of the thousands of people at the conference had filled out an application. It was the first time I learned that God often does not work with the most qualified, but with the most available.

Soon after that, I was assigned to work in Poland and to travel throughout six Communist countries, training groups of young believers in the foundations of the Bible. After completing international ministry training a year later, I moved to Eastern Europe. For the next three years I cut my spiritual teeth in a foreign land. I learned a difficult language, bore the loneliness that came from being cut off from family and friends in a Communist country, and worked with college students who were passionate to study the Word of God.

I was merely a small brick in the foundation of a ministry that eventually reached countless thousands for Christ, but that one choice to follow Him transformed my life into a spiritual adventure. My determination to follow hard after God, to make decisions based on faith, and to seek to be a part of His Kingdom work was the pathway that transformed the rest of my life.

In fact, being challenged to live every day as though it might be my last has made an immense difference throughout my life. "Seeking first the Kingdom of God" became a life focus. Knowing I have only one life to live, one opportunity to invest it fully in the Kingdom of God, has given energy and purpose to each day and every season of my life.

Owning my life means taking responsibility for my own behavior, decisions, and attitudes so I may become all God created me to be and leave a legacy that points others to Him.

While at that first staff training conference, I began to understand what "owning" my life really entails. It means taking responsibility for my own behavior, decisions, and attitudes so I may fully embrace God's amazing vision for my life and leave a legacy that points others to Him. Quite simply, owning my life means living up to my spiritual potential.

I understood very clearly that life is indeed a vapor. Making possessions, accomplishments, or influence my heart's treasures would be a waste of time and energy. Instead, I determined to take God at His word, to risk living beyond my circumstances, and to lean into His call.

Over time, I would formulate a series of questions, or a grid, that I've turned back to again and again as I've tried to evaluate the legacy of faith I'm leaving.

Am I being intentional?

Am I making decisions based on biblical values?

Am I choosing the pathways that will create deep, loving relationships and give value to the people personally connected to me?

Am I willing to take risks of faith to invest my life in the things of eternity?

Am I listening to the world or to the voice of God?

Am I living with Christ and His life as the pattern for my own life?

Do I see this day, these circumstances, as a place in which I can fulfill God's will?

Even now, these questions help me evaluate whether I've really abandoned my life to God. As I look ahead to the next decade of my life, I have been praying, "God, in the power of the Holy Spirit, what do You want me to dream for You? How do You want me to serve? What work do You have for me to do?"

I don't know whether your world has been impacted by a life-altering storm like that flood. If it has, perhaps you've already been forced to face the question of how to live with true purpose. But even if you haven't experienced such a cataclysmic event, I suspect that the deepest part of you longs to live a life that matters. After all, Scripture tells us that God "has planted eternity in the human heart" (Ecclesiastes 3:11, NLT).

The first question all of us who consider the claims of Christ must answer is this: Will we live for God's Kingdom, or will we live for ourselves? As a young Christian, I had no doubt that I wanted to devote my life to Christ. Years later, I can look back and see God's fingerprints all over my life. One reason I wrote this book, in fact, is to let you in on the lessons I've learned as I have tried to follow hard after God. I want to encourage you to live intentionally, too—to make choices from bold faith and generous love that will make a lasting impact.

The keys to living a life of purpose aren't all that mysterious—they're spiritual principles found in the Bible. Yet they must be followed intentionally with the understanding that God has hidden potential in your spiritual DNA. That potential is like a seed waiting to be planted into the circumstances of your life. When you commit to following God through your attitude and actions, that seed will sprout and you will begin to thrive.

Remember—it's not just *possible* to live a full, flourishing life; God actually *designed* you to live this way. At sixty years old, I can look back and see that God has honored those decisions I made to live a life set apart for Him beyond what I ever imagined. I'm grateful that I embraced these values when I was young, but you can begin investing your life for His Kingdom at any age. God is always ready to respond to the one who listens to His call: "The eyes of the LORD search the whole earth in order to strengthen those whose hearts are fully committed to him" (2 Chronicles 16:9, NLT).

Your Life Matters! Live It with Intention!

Have you known people who seem to be alive with the reality of Christ and the winsome ways of His love? Like everyone else, their lives are filled with stresses, challenges, and difficulties, yet somehow they rise above their circumstances and live with the tangible reality of God's blessing and favor. They exude confidence and a willingness to live with risk because of their faith in Him. They are morally strong, spiritually vibrant, and emotionally resilient.

Many of us begin with that same passionate desire to follow Jesus wholeheartedly, only to discover that circumstances sometimes make it difficult to live out that commitment. Hearts broken from the disappointments that come in a fallen world or from burdensome life tasks are often accompanied by depression and discouragement. We all feel this way at times.

In such situations, we may assume that the circumstances of our lives define the spiritual condition of our relationship with God. Often in this place, our lives become filled with mediocrity and compromise. In the end, we may not even live all that differently from those who do not know Christ. Struggles weigh us down and silence any expression of faith. Often, we live as victims of our circumstances instead of mounting up over the difficulties in our lives. We may be troubled because we feel far from God, but our lives are so busy that we never stop to ponder how to change things.

I know how easy it is to start out strong—full of vibrant faith and firm resolve to live for Christ. In fact, as a young woman, I imagined I would give boldly and perhaps even make one big sacrifice, like dying for Jesus after standing up in a great public arena to give testimony of the relevance of the gospel. As a staff member with an international ministry in Communist Eastern Europe, I enjoyed seeing God work in dramatic ways. I also lived as a single woman, wondering if I would ever get married.

Then just a few years later, I was a young wife and mother back in the States. Life became monotonous and ordinary. Could God still use me? I thought about the common men and women whom Christ had called, the ones He challenged to drop their fishing nets, tax-collecting businesses, and normal lives to follow Him. Because those first-century believers were faithful and partnered with God, the gospel of Christ went all over the world in one generation, without the Internet, without phones, without televisions. Person to person, parent to child, neighbor to neighbor, these sold-out men and women delivered powerful, look-me-in-the-eye messages that resulted in transformed lives.

When I imagine the first followers of Jesus, I often think of the disciples who accompanied Him in His ministry. These are the men and women who willingly journeyed far from home to spread the gospel, and many eventually gave up their lives for Him. Yet I've come to the realization that many of those who followed Christ did not leave their communities. Some were called to be quiet radicals who provided the meals, homes, and finances that enabled the twelve apostles to keep going. Others took care of their children and whispered Kingdom messages into those little ones' souls. Some prayed or taught other believers in their homes, or cared for sick and handicapped relatives, bringing joy and beauty to their lives every day.

There is no single way to serve God, but the point is this: We each have only one life to live to tell a story about Him, about His ways, about His love. And if we are Christ followers, then God calls us to use our gifts, to exercise our faith, and to become salt and light right where we are.

For most of us, spirituality is a long-term work of service carried out in ordinary days. For me, it's a moment-by-moment choice to put aside my own needs and selfish desires to give one more time— to grocery shop and cook for guests; to listen to someone in pain; to attend to my garden so that it brings beauty to those who sit on my front porch; to cook one more healthy meal and wash the dirty dishes afterward with a thankful heart; to pay bills; to stay up late with a teenager; to work hard to meet one more deadline. Lasting love and influence for the gospel happen in the hidden moments of life when only God sees my heart and my faithfulness.

Lasting love and influence for the gospel happen in the hidden moments of life.

Until we accept God's desire to work powerfully through even the most ordinary people, we may settle for humdrum lives, missing the opportunities that God places all around us to make a lasting impact. The first three chapters of this book examine some of the barriers that prevent many women from living all out for His Kingdom.

Once we understand our identity as women redeemed by Christ and created with meaningful purpose, we can start to map out our specific life mission. We'll look at how we begin that process in part 2. In the next section, we'll acknowledge a few of the mysterious ways in which God empowers us—but only when we open ourselves up to His transforming work. Owning our lives is not a passive exercise, however; we must choose to embrace, with God's help, certain attitudes and actions that enable us to give all of ourselves to Him. We'll explore those in part 4. The final section of the book centers on the ultimate purpose of all of our lives: to love well. When we own our lives, we choose to make love the priority in our homes, our marriages, and our parenting. From it flows the very legacy that God created us to fulfill.

Each chapter concludes with a section I call "Own Your Part." Here you'll find discussion questions and exercises designed to help you make the most of your own life. I wish I could personally sit down with all my readers so we could learn from and encourage each other, but since that isn't possible, I've ended each chapter with the prayer I would offer if we were meeting together.

When my children were young, I would tell them, "I believe God has given you the capacity and the ability to grow strong inside, to live courageously, to have great faith, and to become a person of considerable influence in your lifetime. God has made you with such wonderful potential. But I cannot make you strong and good—you will have to choose that for yourself. I will love you, encourage you, and help you in every way. But I cannot make you a great person.

"You will have to decide that you want to be excellent of character and then make the hard decisions to become the best you can be, to follow hard after God, and to live into your potential. You have a choice to make!"

Similarly, God has created you with the potential to live a purposeful, meaningful life that is spiritually strong and vibrant. But you have to choose to follow Him, to believe Him, to live for Him. You must choose how to live every day.

Own your life. Choose whom you will serve. Live into Christ's love and the power of His Spirit working through you.

If you follow hard after Him, God will make your life count in ways you can't even yet see. May you be blessed in the chasing after Him in your own life, and may you see evidence of His strong support for you because you have given your heart completely to Him.

PART 1

Barriers to Owning Your Life

Don't Settle for a Mediocre Life

CHAPTER 1

SEEING BEAUTY AND PURPOSE IN YOUR ORDINARY DAYS

Owning the Hero Who Lives inside You

What distinguishes men of genuine achievement from the rest of us is not so much their intellectual powers and aptitudes as their curiosity, their energy, their fullest use of their potentialities. Nobody really knows how smart or talented he is until he finds the incentives to use himself to the fullest. God has given us more than we know what to do with. SYDNEY J. HARRIS

The people who know their God will display strength and take action.
DANIEL 11:32

STANDING TO MY FULL HEIGHT, I pranced down the imaginary platform in my den, acting out the time when I would be crowned Miss America. As with many girls born in the 1950s, watching this contest on television had become a yearly ritual. Even as a little girl posing as a beauty queen, I knew in my heart I was born to become someone significant.

Reading books about heroes of history further fed these dreams. Whether Florence Nightingale, braving the filthy trenches of war to save lives, or Madame Curie, who helped pave the way for new cancer treatments, I was right there with them in the story, visualizing how I would help save my world in some small way.

Fast-forward a couple of decades, when I found myself squishing next to my seven-year-old son on a couch, munching chocolate chip cookies and sharing a "little boy" moment.

"Mama, you know what? I think Superman was just like Jesus. He came from a far-off place to save his world. I think I am going to be Superman when I grow up because I am going to do something to save my world."

Sitting up straighter with his chest puffed out, Nathan said, "You know what? Superman is inside me just waiting to come out!"

Perhaps all children anticipate how they might fulfill some great destiny in their lifetimes. *I believe there is also a heroine in each of our hearts waiting to come out.* Yet somewhere along the pathway of our lives, we lose our innocence, forget our dreams, and succumb to a life filled with monotony and responsibility. I remember pondering this very thought when I was a young wife and mother feeling "stuck" at a particular moment. I wondered how I had gotten there, since I had always hoped to do something of significance.

As a young adult, mission work had taken me to many exciting cities. I had moved to Communist countries throughout Eastern Europe, meeting secretly with people to teach them the truths of the Bible and to train them to share faith in their own countries.

As a single missionary, I lived in Vienna, Krakow, and Warsaw. After Clay and I married, we moved to Vienna and then worked in Long Beach, Denver, and Nashville. Being a part of so many urban communities gave me a taste for city life. Having friends from many backgrounds and cultures brought me great pleasure and stimulation. A charming coffee shop was always just a fifteen-minute walk or drive away. We regularly dined at cafés and restaurants with international cuisine, but our lives were about to drastically change.

When our children were young, Clay and I began dreaming of starting a publishing company and family ministry. To fulfill that vision, we moved with our three oldest children, who were eleven, eight, and six, from Nashville to my mother-in-law's house. Our new home was located in a tiny town of 712 people, forty-five minutes away from the nearest grocery store with fresh food or a loaf of whole grain bread.

Life in this tiny old town left me feeling disoriented and frustrated. The temperature surpassed one hundred degrees almost every day, and chiggers—those tiny bugs—chewed on my children and me every time we went outdoors, leaving countless itching bumps. The only place to shop was a little convenience store two miles away in town (and it smelled like grease from all the fried chicken sold there). We had no babysitters, no friends, not even a church or library—and the graduating class at the local school was seven in a good year. There was no coffee shop or café—and we didn't have money to afford eating out anyway. Paying for groceries, clothing, and doctors' bills devoured our small income. Goodwill and secondhand stores were my only shopping options, and then only if we had a few dollars left at the end of the month and could make the long drive to a bigger town.

My mother-in-law's house was laid out in such a way that our kids could make a circular path through it—starting in the living room, going through our bedroom, then continuing through the hallway to the kitchen, and finally reaching the living room again. Round and round they would run! One day, not long before I had my fourth child, I was sitting on the floor of our bedroom in front of a small couch. I guess I was hidden from the children's view because when they ran their standard route, they came in one door and went out the other while calling, "Mama, Mama, where are you?"

When I realized they couldn't see me, but only the back of the couch, I did not answer. There I was, an adult in my early forties, hiding behind the couch and hoping my children would not find me. As I sat on the floor, I was Eeyore living under clouds of "Woe is me."

My mind scanned the past year and came up with a number of disturbing memories: my two miscarriages (one in which I had almost died); the packed boxes and messes all around us; our regular encounters with spiders or snakes; a mother-in-law who hovered and followed me around the house as I worked and cooked; three kids who would not go outside and play in the scorching heat; and the squishy squash bugs on our outside plants in what was supposed to be my country garden. On top of that, I had no nearby friends or support systems and, did I mention, no strong cup of coffee?

More thoughts came: My family wanted to eat so often, and they made so many messes every day. This was not at all how I'd envisioned my life. I considered myself a professional, adult sort of person, not a pregnant forty-two-year-old mama with secondhand clothes who was throwing up and sweating through life with children and messes all around me.

In that moment, my life was a pile of puzzle pieces, all mixed up with no seeming pattern or logical way to fit them together. And a heroine was not to be found in the picture. As I scrutinized the landscape of my soul, I saw endless darkness down a gloomy hallway that seemed to end in despair. Nothing in my life seemed to be matching up with my ideals; I was physically, spiritually, and emotionally drained, and everyone and everything depended on my keeping it all together. This place was as far from an adventure requiring heroism as I could imagine.

Add to that, a number of critics waited in line to freely voice their opinions to Clay and me.

"Have you lost your mind, moving to such a tiny town? Are you sure this is where you are supposed to be?"

"Ninety-five percent of all new businesses fail the first year, and they end up bankrupt!"

"What experience do you have in publishing? I thought the real publishers already rejected your book ideas—what makes you think you can publish them yourselves and find anyone who wants to hear what you have to say?"

Then there were the warnings from family—"You know, someday you are going to have to get a job that pays real money. You can't just fiddle around your whole life. You need to think of your children and how you are raising them!"

And "After three miscarriages—one you almost died from—you are pregnant again? You are tempting fate. If something more serious happens, it will be your own fault."

"I think it is fine if you homeschool your children when they are young because you can't mess them up too badly. But what about when they're older? What will you do then about your children's education when the nearest big school is in another county, miles and miles away? And have you considered that they won't get the socialization they need?"

It was while juggling these pressures on our marriage, finances, spiritual life, family life, and ideals that I felt breathless with fear and insecurity as I hid behind that couch. It was then that I had a big "come to Jesus meeting."

Tears flowed down my face uncontrollably. Miraculously, no one found me.

"God," I whispered, "I have served you faithfully for many years. What am I doing here? Life is so hard. This place doesn't suit my personality. And my mother-in-law is no Naomi. Does it really matter that I have served you as best I know how all of these years? How can any good come out of these circumstances? I don't think I can make it here. Please take me out of this situation."

Escape. That was my first line of defense when I was in this very rough place. Where could I go to get away from these problems?

Looking back, I realize my response was pretty typical. We live in a culture of runaways—rushing to another marriage, job, house, Internet thrill, vacation, drug, whatever. Yet when we run away all the time, our "demons"—the problems, difficult relationships, scars, fears, insecurity, selfishness—seem to follow us. Ironically, the very difficulties we want to escape can be overcome only when we face them head-on. Otherwise, they have a way of following us wherever we go. Not only that, but running away from them keeps us from growing stronger and eventually becoming heroes in our own stories.

After I said my brief prayer and spilled all my tears, quietness came. The sun was setting outside and cast soft shadows in our room. Finally, the kids had gone outside to play with the dogs.

The comfort of God's Spirit gently began to blow through me, as I was finally ready to open my heart in humility and prayer. A little song my children had been listening to pressed upon my mind: "This is the day that the Lord has made. I will rejoice and be glad in it."

This day, this place, these circumstances—God had made them!

The Lord seemed to speak to me from all the devotions I had been having with my little ones, and a verse came to my mind: "All discipline for the moment seems not to be joyful, but sorrowful; yet to those who have been trained by it, afterwards it yields the peaceful fruit of righteousness" (Hebrews 12:11).

The very difficulties we want to escape can be overcome only when we face them head-on.

The words that captured my attention were "those who have been *trained* by it." Training is something that is repeated again and again over a long period of time, in order to build strength and endurance. God wanted to train me in holiness right where I was, in these circumstances.

Then I felt Him impress the following on my heart: *Sally, this is the place I want you to worship Me. Being faithful in these circumstances is where you will find the glory of My favor. This is exactly where I want you. This time of testing will be the making of your faith, the humbling of your heart, the shaping of your character, the writing of your story. You can choose to waste this time with a bad attitude, to leave this situation, or to waste your days in ungratefulness and complaints. And then your life will continue moving through darkness and dim hallways.*

You have a choice to make: If you trust Me and live faithfully in this juncture, I will make this a place of favor and honor for you. But if you look for a way out and disqualify yourself from the blessings and favor I had planned to give you, you will find yourself in the midst of a prolonged wilderness.

And so the itchy, green shag carpet behind the tiny, worn loveseat that hid me from view became an altar of worship for me. *Lord, I will choose to find light in this darkness. I have no guarantee about how any of this will turn out, but I am planting a flag of faith. No matter what happens, I will be as obedient as I can to bring joy into this place, to create beauty in this wilderness, to exercise generous love, and to persevere with patience. I will choose to believe that wherever You are my faithful companion is the place where Your blessing will be upon me.*

Peace clothed me like an embrace from God. I had been tested and had come through with grace. This was only one of many dark and difficult junctures on my life pathway, and yet I was now learning to ask at each turn in the road, "What is the lesson here, God? What wisdom can I learn? How can I bring grace, beauty, and order to each day, and live as though it is a place of worship?"

Later that evening, I committed my thoughts to my journal, writing down life goals that would help determine the kind of woman I would become in the years ahead. I resolved:

> to be a joyful person
> to practice being thankful
> to see God's fingerprints each day of my life, as I knew my
>   children probably longed to have a happy mother
> to live every day by faith, choosing to believe that God was real,
>   that He listened to prayer, and that He would provide the
>   grace to get through every trial
> to love, as much as possible, all of those who came into my life

Finally, I committed to work hard and to grow in strength, as I was beginning to understand that living up to these ideals would require a lifetime of working, cooking, cleaning, writing, living, teaching, and speaking.

Reflecting on Sixty Years of Walking with God

Hindsight does indeed bring great insight. Though there are some images I'd still rather forget from that time—such as the scorpion that fell from the ceiling and stung me on the thigh when I was 9½ months pregnant (and even then the baby would not come!). And yet it was in that remote house in a tiny town that my children learned to love the country, living wild and free in the place I first thought cursed. The time with fewer friends, distractions, and lessons, though often lonely, drew our family circle closer together than ever would have happened if we had been in a large city with limitless choices.

My marriage grew stronger because I was forced to be less self-ish and to believe in the dreams of my husband. My compassion for those who were lonely, who lived on little income, and who were forced to overcome seemingly impossible circumstances grew out of the humility that developed as I waited on God in faith. My ministry messages grew out of my life experiences.

These were the memories I pondered as I sipped the warm cup of tea my daughter Joy brought me on the morning of my sixtieth birthday. Her instructions as she met me coming down the stairs from my bedroom had been, "Mom, we have a whole day of celebration prepared for you. But I want to give you a few minutes alone first while we finish cooking breakfast so you can ponder all those sixty years. That way we can hear the stories and celebrate all the meaning-ful days with you today!"

And so I did take some time to sift through my memories. As I wrote in the introduction, I had been challenged early in life to live every day as though it were my last. Now I asked myself, *Have I lived into the spiritual reality of the God who brought me to Himself? Have I written a story of faith and faithfulness that will speak inspiration to generations to come?*

As I reflected on the years, the first inklings of the thoughts that led me to write this book developed. I realized that God had been faithful and that I had lived a life sprinkled with His favor, miracles, and blessing. I wanted to share, from a perspective of deep grateful-ness and gathered wisdom, some of the spiritual secrets I had learned about how to live a flourishing life.

I also had come to understand and appreciate the ways God had taught me. Many of the years I spent serving Him with my whole heart had been invisible to the public. I had not lived a perfect life. At times, I resisted the very pressures that God wanted to use to train me to become strong. But I could see that when I yielded to His ways and lived with His hand holding mine, my life story had become more than I could ever have imagined.

I know now that heroes come with a variety of stories. A radical life for Christ is not always visible to outside eyes. Even Jesus lived in a tiny town, never venturing more than fifty miles from His home during His ministry. Though He did not work with great world leaders and was obscure in His commonness, Christ's love and service literally changed the history of the world. So many of my own years had been poured into the mundane moments of life, yet I sought to make each one a celebration of His reality.

Through seventeen moves (six international), car accidents, illnesses, church splits, seven pregnancies, three miscarriages, four children, and even a house fire, life had indeed been an adventure. God had been my companion throughout, and He had enabled me to emerge with a legacy of His faithfulness.

My sixty years had been sprinkled with small miracles, hard work, endless days of faith through the darkness, and so many moments of pleasure and deep blessings of love. I thought of my marriage of thirty-three years, and how my husband and I had come to understand the real meaning of love and commitment. The hard work of our marriage had shaped each of us, one humble day after the other, to become more understanding, more accepting, more thankful for each other than we ever could have been when we started. Of course our lives had been fraught with the pettiness of our own selfishness and, at times, loneliness, and yet we had persevered and made it through the years with such a meaningful heritage of family.

A radical life for Christ is not always visible to outside eyes.

What a blessing to have dreamed together about becoming message makers to strengthen families. After thousands of hours of work, we had built a ministry together, written a number of books, started a publishing house, and seen our books translated into eight languages.

And what a miracle to have been able to parent, having no

experience with children and no natural patience for all the work it required. We had not only faced the challenges of living in a remote location but had also faced severe bouts of asthma, OCD, learning challenges, and all the difficulties that naturally come as a result of children's inherent selfishness. Yet thirty years into parenting, I rejoiced as I thought about my children: four vibrant, beautiful adults who cared about life, loved us, and were committed to faithfully serving God.

The grid through which I had lived my life was based on my understanding that in order to live a flourishing life of influence, I had to own my life—to take responsibility for my choices, attitude, will, and actions, knowing they would all have consequences for eternity. Once I understood that my integrity was built when no one but Christ was looking, I was motivated to remain faithful in moments alone with Him and my Bible.

The moment so many years ago in our bedroom at my mother-in-law's house, when I had felt trapped in the wilderness of life, had been a turning point. The desert years, in fact, had become the deepest blessing of my life.

There I learned that life was not about my ease, but about God's desire to help me become mature. He wanted to take from my hands the very things I was holding on to for security so that I could find lasting happiness in the simple things that could never be lost—the breathtaking beauty of a wilderness sunset; the contentment that my children learned from having few toys and only the open land in which to pretend and play; the soul-satisfying relationships that develop in a family who have only one another to rely on; and the gratification that comes from learning to be happy apart from material possessions.

Perhaps most important, I discovered that heroes are made during the secret moments. Though they practice faith, integrity, and courage when no one else is there to see, at the right time, they will come out of spiritual "basic training" with the integrity and action required to accomplish something great.

Putting Together the Pieces of Your Unique Life Puzzle

Each of us has a different life puzzle to assemble. The choices you make in the midst of your life journey do have eternal consequences. Yes, you can throw the pieces at God in anger and say, "I do not like the life You have given me, and I refuse to live within these limitations with a humble heart. You have made me a victim. You have ruined my life. I will choose to live in darkness." If that is your choice, the puzzle of your life will remain fragmented and separated, with holes in the picture.

However, if you choose to bow your knee and submit to the varied circumstances of your life, God will do miracles. If you choose to trust and develop your integrity and an inner standard of holiness that isn't dependent on cultural standards, the puzzle pieces will begin to come together. No matter what your limitations are—health issues, financial problems, a difficult marriage or divorce, a loss of friendship, death of a dream—your life is meant to be filled to the brim with the potential of God's blessings. But in order to thrive and heal, you must accept any limitations by faith, trust in His faithfulness each step of the way, and wait for His grace so you can live a faithful story right in the place you find yourself.

If you embrace your unique puzzle of life, you will find wholeness. As you look to God to slowly figure out how to put the pieces together, you will see a beautiful picture emerge. Your story lived faithfully will become your glory—the place where He builds messages, provides answers to prayer, and teaches wisdom.

❋

Own Your Part

I have a collection of teacups and mugs. Each is different in size, shape, and color—but every one of them is functional and beloved by my family. In the same way, each of our lives is unique. Our differences do not devalue our intrinsic worth, but they do create a different design. I have always told my children, "You might as well decide to like God's will for your life, since your circumstances are probably not going to change just because you wish they would."

1. What defines and makes your life distinct? What resources do you have? What do you consider to be advantages to your particular puzzle? Are there any areas that seem impossible at this moment that you need to put into God's hands?

    We know that God causes all things to work together for good to those who love God, to those who are called according to His purpose.   ROMANS 8:28

    How does the verse above apply to your own life right now?

2. Learning to see each turn in the road and each unique circumstance as a part of what God has ordained has helped me find purpose at each juncture. I ask Him, *Lord, what can I learn from this? What message at this moment might prepare me to encourage someone in the same circumstances later? Show me Your faithfulness now so I can keep learning.*

    Trust in the LORD and do good;
    Dwell in the land and cultivate faithfulness.   PSALM 37:3

    This verse has helped me learn to stay in the moment and grow where I am. How is God asking you to be faithful wherever you are today? What does it mean to cultivate faithfulness?

Praying with You

Lord, each of us finds challenges in each season of our lives. Help us today to cultivate faithfulness right where we are. Give us the spiritual eyes to believe that You will work this situation out for our good. We come in Jesus' name. Amen.

CHAPTER 2

CONTROLLING THE CHAOS

Owning Your Priorities and Commitments

*You will never have a greater or lesser dominion than that over yourself
. . . the height of a man's success is gauged by his self-mastery; the depth of his
failure by his self-abandonment. . . . And this law is the expression of eternal
justice. He who cannot establish dominion over himself will have no dominion
over others.* LEONARDO DA VINCI

*Thus says the LORD,
    "What injustice did your fathers find in Me,
    That they went far from Me
    And walked after emptiness and became empty?"* JEREMIAH 2:5

TREKKING ALONG with the crowds of people hurrying to work in downtown New York City, I looked anxiously for the café meeting place for an auspicious gathering of Christian publishers and writers. Because I considered myself a work-from-my–living room, coffee-drinking, comfy clothes–wearing writer, I wondered if I would seem out of place in this group. In an attempt to hide my insecurity and look as professional and intelligent as possible, I made a point of arriving early.

Soon I was sitting among a group of seven women who were all wearing dark business suits and boots. We sat chatting and laughing as we launched into "writers' conversation." Before long, we had settled in for a rousing discussion while eating forkfuls of Italian cuisine. Fifteen minutes after our appointed meeting time, a young woman with a cell phone grasped to her ear rushed breathlessly into the room.

She looked slightly disheveled, and in her dash to the table, her brief-case fell to the floor, papers scattering. After quickly ending her call and gathering her belongings, she said, "I'm so sorry I am late. Today, all of the chaos consumed me and left me empty."

The older execs in the room raised their eyebrows; the younger writers smiled. Her words—"The chaos consumed me and left me empty"—haunted me. Isn't that the way many of us feel? Pulling up a chair, the young woman asked my permission to sit next to me. After we'd enjoyed a long lunch talking about book ideas, the exhausted young woman turned to me and said, "If you could write a book about how to have peace in the midst of the chaos of everyday life, you would sell a gazillion books. That is how everyone I know is living—in utter, busy chaos!"

I wanted to tell her that she didn't need to find peace in the chaos; instead, she needed to move, step-by-step, toward a more reasonable and centered life. Owning your life, you may remember, means taking responsibility for your actions and attitudes. What this writer and so many other women don't realize is that God has equipped all of us to live more simply, to move toward order, and to live with intentionality.

This woman was another inspiration as I worked on this book. But the idea of writing about how we can own our lives came long before I met her. As a conference speaker and mentor to a number of young bloggers, I have watched many women battle compulsive busyness. I have also received a growing number of letters, e-mails, and Facebook messages from women who feel angry, discouraged, defeated, hopeless, or lonely.

My counsel to all of those crying out for help: In order to move from chaos to order, we must each make a plan that will move us away from a never-ending flurry of activities toward God's design for our lives. That plan begins by identifying the drainers and sources of chaos that steal our spiritual and emotional energy. To move forward, in other words, we must first recognize what is holding us back. Only then can we reset the patterns in our lives.

Identifying the Chaos

No matter where I go, women tell me they are "way too busy." The busyness and distractions keep ramping up, which means there is always more to do, leading to exhaustion and a sense of always being behind. Between frenzied activity and the peer pressure to constantly do more, many women's deepest needs are being ignored.

What little time remains is often stolen by the Internet and social media—outlets that seem to promise connection but often waste our time without offering the gratification we long to experience. Freeways, fast food, and a constant barrage of television, movies, and media feed

Busyness falsely promises productivity.

our frenzy for more "stuff" and convenience without providing the connection to community and deeper friendship we long for. Instead, we often simply feel guilty and inadequate.

The end result? Depression and isolation. Many women wonder how they will get off the merry-go-round of life. Even in Christian circles, women live with deep weariness and what I call sawdust souls—an inability to experience any lasting joy. Their spirits are dry and depleted, but they aren't even sure how to get close to God, or how to have intimacy with family and friends.

Often, there is subtle confusion about how life "got" this way. Nonstop activity is a cultural badge of honor that supposedly means a person is making progress. Busyness falsely promises productivity. Frankly, our culture encourages us to take on more and more, and busyness and distraction can be addicting.

Yet we are drifting further from the life God designed us to live. Surely this is not the abundant life God promised. Is there a better way to find purpose and satisfaction?

Looking back in time reveals that our problems are not unique. The Old Testament prophet Jeremiah lived in a day when people substituted the ideals of God with the values of their culture. In fact, many themes in Jeremiah are familiar to us: sexual promiscuity, neglect of the family, materialism and acquiring wealth while ignoring the poor, and adopting the "forms" of religion without growing closer to God.

Jeremiah 2:5 records God's response to such a culture:

> Thus says the LORD,
>   "What injustice did your fathers find in Me,
>   That they went far from Me
>   And walked after emptiness and became empty?"

The phrase that caught my attention was the final one: They "walked after emptiness and became empty." This seems such a fitting description of the times in which we live.

Walking after something refers to the paths we take and the places we go. Unless we radically change our way of life and the direction we are taking, we cannot live into the ways of God. Instead of the peace and purpose He promises, we will find only emptiness.

Throughout Scripture, God warns us against developing idols. In our sophistication, we do not think of ourselves as idolatrous people, as we do not worship statues or look to them to give us meaning and protection. Yet can you identify with any of the ways so many of us waste our lives?

> Seeking the pleasure of things that fill our homes but bring
>   no meaning
> Working incessantly and storing up wealth in an attempt to
>   control the security of our lives, while being exhausted in
>   the pursuit
> Entertaining ourselves to death by the endless hours we give our
>   hearts and minds to television and computer, feeling empty
>   at the end

What are your idols, or the habits that steal your heart? What consumes your energy, time, focus, and money and takes away from time pursuing God? What do you hold on to that you hope will make you happy and bring fulfillment? What are the empty pursuits of your own life? Until you identify those areas that unnecessarily rob you of time, you will continue on the hamster wheel endlessly.

In the end, remember this: Nothing in this world will fill the deep crevices of your life with peace, contentment, love, and joy except God.

Recognizing the Voices That Influence You

Media has convinced us that we need a big home, the right car, a certain body type, and luxurious experiences to truly enjoy life. Advertising makes us long for belongings, adventures, and ideas that most people throughout world history never possessed or even imagined. The proliferation of voices with access to our brains builds a barrier against what God has promised—real, valuable, and lasting fulfillment.

Nothing in this world will fill the deep crevices of your life with peace, contentment, love, and joy except God.

Most women I meet do not truly even have a basis or background to understand the Word of God. And without that knowledge, our decisions and direction will be guided by the world's "wisdom." Unless we return to God's original design for us and listen to His wisdom, the confusing voices of culture, even Christian culture, will lead us astray. As the writer of Proverbs tells us, "He will die for lack of instruction, and in the greatness of his folly he will go astray" (Proverbs 5:23).

Christians must know and understand the foundations of Scripture in order to make biblical choices for their lives. If they follow the values of the world instead, they will die for lack of instruction and stray from the blessing of living by God's truth. In the absence of biblical convictions, people will go the way of culture. Christian culture is often so close to the world's that Christians' values are indistinguishable from the falsehood of worldly philosophy. Without a biblical basis for making choices in life, people will surely become lost.

Building on the Right Foundations

Vast destruction and massive loss of life inevitably seem to result from the typhoons and earthquakes that strike parts of Asia. Yet as the media and relief organizations often point out, these great losses are often due to the poor infrastructure and inadequate foundations of homes throughout the region. Most structures were not built to withstand powerful storms.

Jesus was very clear about building our lives on solid foundations. The Sermon on the Mount, found in Matthew 5–7, is Jesus' longest teaching in the Gospels. This Scripture describes the character and blessings of those who follow Jesus. In this section, Jesus teaches about how to approach God in prayer and to approach others with integrity. Here we learn that those who enter God's Kingdom must enter "through the narrow gate," not the wide-open path most of the world follows. Jesus ends the sermon by saying,

> Everyone who hears these words of Mine and acts on them, may be compared to a wise man who built his house on the rock. And the rain fell, and the floods came, and the winds blew and slammed against that house; and yet it did not fall, for it had been founded on the rock. Everyone who hears these words of Mine and does not act on them, will be like a foolish man who built his house on the sand. The rain fell, and the floods came, and the winds blew and slammed against that house; and it fell—and great was its fall.
>
> MATTHEW 7:24-27

If we build our lives on the foundation of Jesus' words, we will stand strong through all the floods of life. If we do not heed His words and build on the sand of cultural values instead, our lives will fall—and great will be their fall. Pretty simple—if we are not building on His wisdom, our houses will crash. And there is no place in between; we are either building on rock or building on sand.

Paul put it another way when he was teaching Timothy about the end times and the distractions people would follow:

> The time will come when they will not endure sound doctrine; but wanting to have their ears tickled, they will accumulate for themselves teachers in accordance to their own desires, and will turn away their ears from the truth and will turn aside to myths.   2 TIMOTHY 4:3-4

Is it possible we have turned our ears from truth and turned aside to myths—the values and promises of the world that will never fulfill or provide the solid foundations on which to build our lives? I do not know anyone who has said, "I think I will purposely build my whole life on sandy foundations because I intend to allow the investment of my life to fall apart." And yet daily we see the consequences of unwise choices creating havoc in the lives of those who call themselves Christians.

We often see mediocrity and compromise in the lives of leaders. Many pastors have compromised their marriages through immorality. Christian businessmen and women have been known to cheat and invest illegally. The divorce rate is high, addiction to pornography is epidemic, and sexual promiscuity is rampant. Why is that? Many of us struggle to bring God's light to influence culture; instead, we have allowed culture to inform our values, our work ethic, and our ideals. Consequently, the values and habits of the world and Christians' choices are often indistinguishable.

Out of thousands of letters I have received, these are common statements:

> "I feel desperate and out of control of my life almost every day
>   and don't know what to do."
> "I am so lonely and isolated and wish I had more friends. As
>   a result, I became addicted to the Internet, and now I can't

stop spending hours online every day—even though I still feel lonely."

"I just couldn't stay married any longer. My spouse bored me."

"The daily news of a sinking economy, rising taxes, wars, and government's failure leaves me fearful and despondent. I am afraid for my children's future. I feel powerless."

"I knew I should never have slept with him, but he told me he loved me, and I believed him. Now that I am pregnant, he doesn't want anything to do with me."

"I yell at my children every day and feel guilty, but I don't like being a mom. They take too much time."

"I wish I could be a good parent to my children, but I had a broken family background, and I don't even know where to start!"

"I quit going to church because I couldn't find one that inspired me or met my needs."

So why the "disconnect" between God's design and the impotence of most people's lives? Most of us do not have a corpus of Scripture in our minds, a comprehensive understanding of the Bible and its truths that can counteract the voices of culture. Yet in order to build well, we must have the right resources—a growing understanding and obedience to the words and messages of the God who created us.

Without a biblical basis for making choices in life, people will surely become lost. We were all born with the capacity to live effective lives, but culture has lost an imagination for godly character that produces such lives.

God always intended that we live a life full of meaning and fulfillment. His very imprint on our lives means that we are to live with excellence in every area—we should be better lovers, more industrious workers, greater teachers, more generous givers, more profound thinkers, the finest cooks, the most skillful artists. In short, we have the capacity—God's very stamp on our souls—to be a reflection of Him in and through every part of our lives.

We were made for love—in fact, loving God and loving others sums up all the law! When a Pharisee asked Jesus, "Teacher, which is the greatest commandment in the Law?" Christ responded,

> "You shall love the LORD your God with all your heart,
> and with all your soul, and with all your mind." . . . The
> second is like it, "You shall love your neighbor as yourself."
> On these two commandments depend the whole Law
> and the Prophets. MATTHEW 22:36-40

Our calling is to bring light—like Jesus—so that when we step into the worlds of others, we bring His peace to every person and enlighten the dark places of the world. Coming into contact with us should be like coming into contact with Jesus. And in fulfilling these purposes, we find satisfaction and peace in our souls.

We have a longing for more because we were created for more! Our hearts tell us we were crafted for an eternal place, for courage, for ideals that draw the best from our existence. Epic movies capture our imagination because of our desire to be a part of an epic story ourselves. We were made to be heroes in our own stories.

Returning to God's design and understanding His instruction book for how we were made to live are both essential. The goal of this book is to help Christians own their lives. That requires taking responsibility for our decisions and understanding that each person has the power and authority to bring his or her life back into order. Each of us is a steward of the days allotted for our lifetime, and learning to manage our commitments and priorities is critical.

We can become empowered Christians who live meaningful
    lives.
We can love generously and have relationships that satisfy.
We can leave the past behind and own a life without
    condemnation.

We are made to accomplish great feats of faith and courage and
to live a life worth telling.

Through the Holy Spirit, we can live strategic, flourishing lives. The
map to get us there requires only that we focus on the values and goals
of Scripture so that we may take back the ground that has been lost.

We were created for so much more—more life, more power to
influence our circumstances, more strength through the power of the
Holy Spirit to overcome our circumstances and to bring light into
dark places of our lives.

Mastering Your Will

Mastering your will is the secret to living within His design and owning your life again. In other words, choosing to obey the prompting
of God to live with righteous choices—and recognizing your ability to
exert your own decision or will to live in response to His Word—is the
pathway to growing spiritually strong.

As the old saying goes, "Where there is a will, there is a way."
Each of us has a "will" inside that determines, to a great degree, how
strong we will become in living abundant, flourishing lives. How you
exercise your choices, how you choose to invest your mind, and the
degree to which you exert self-discipline to follow through with wise
decisions will determine the fruit of your life.

Stewarding your life wisely can bring great confidence, excellence
of character, and peace of mind—and lead you to create a legacy, a
story worth telling. But it begins with a determination on your part to
make a wise plan, to forge reasonable goals, to listen to the prompting
of the Holy Spirit, and to trust God to lead you on a path of spiritual
renewal and strength.

Each day, you are writing the story that your life will tell throughout eternity. As you recommit to God's values and priorities, every
choice you make and every action you take will move you toward the
exceptional life for which you were made.

*

Own Your Part

Before a great house is built, an architect must design an extensive plan that considers the beauty of the structure; the practical application of electrical, plumbing, and heating elements for the home; and the aesthetic appeal for those living in the home. Any great structure requires great planning. So it is with life. In order to build a vibrant spiritual life, intentional plans must be made. Planning for the practical issues, the spiritual goals, and the dreams to accomplish comes through intentional and purposeful consideration.

Before you read the next chapter, take the following actions to help build a solid plan for your life:

1. Identify the chaos in your life.

What activities or relationships create the most havoc? Steal your energy? Produce life-noise that keeps you from quiet and peace?

2. Recognize the voices.

Name the voices that are influencing your decisions and the commitments that are leading you away from a centered life or promising false gratification.

Ask yourself who or what is influencing your decisions and if they are worthy of following.

Determine to begin writing down the goals and decisions that will lead you to a wiser stewardship of life.

3. Build on the right foundations.

Identify worldly values that have taken your money, time, and heart commitment. Where might you begin investing those resources to build your life on what matters?

Make a plan to incorporate back into your life the ideals that lead to real relationships and eternal values and that will fill you up emotionally, spiritually, and mentally.

Control your schedule by eliminating time wasters. Schedule a daily time when you can begin to read and study the Word of God.

4. Master your will.

Identify the areas of your life that you have neglected or ignored and that you know will bring you more health (e.g., better time management, devotions, personal relationships, health, church).

Write down the ways you would like to grow in each of the areas you identified. Then set small goals toward moving in that direction.

Praying with You

Lord, so often we are overwhelmed by all the tasks ahead of us. Today help us to turn our eyes to You so that we can discern between the truly important tasks and those that will not add any real value to our lives. May we look to You as our Peace today. Amen.

CHAPTER 3

LISTENING TO NEW VOICES

Owning Your True Identity

I am a princess. All girls are. Even if they live in tiny old attics. Even if they dress in rags, even if they aren't pretty, or smart, or young. They're still princesses.
FRANCES HODGSON BURNETT, *A LITTLE PRINCESS*

We are His workmanship, created in Christ Jesus for good works, which God prepared beforehand so that we would walk in them.   EPHESIANS 2:10

ONCE IN A GREAT WHILE, I meet a true kindred spirit—someone who gets me, who takes the time to probe my heart, who laughs at the same things, and who knows when to be serious and nod at the right moments as I am sharing my heart.

Not long ago, I discovered such a friend, a surprise gift God gave me after I had complained to Him that afternoon about how I often give out and encourage others while left with a longing for a soul-mate friend of my own. That evening, I met Elizabeth as we sat across from each other at the last dinner of a health seminar we were attending.

"Tell me about yourself," I said as I munched on more raw vegetables.

"I will soon celebrate my sixtieth birthday!" she answered between bites.

"Great age, isn't it?" I said. "I just turned sixty. It's a wonderful time to evaluate and plan your life investment for the coming years. So what would you like to do in the next twenty years?"

"I think I want to start another business!" she responded without missing a beat.

I was drawn to this woman who seemed so alive, so excited about the possibilities of her life as she dreamed about still more adventures.

After we had moved to some couches away from the crowd, we spent the next three hours chatting. As we got to know each other better, we shared some deep places of our hearts—spaces that I rarely open to anyone. She told me how she'd chased some of her own dreams.

"As a little girl, I saw a movie about New York City, and from that moment on, I determined I would move there someday. I wanted to start a business and live in that exciting city, and I did just that!"

She discovered an old New York neighborhood where she started a charming and successful restaurant, which became well known and hosted famous people from all over the world. With her earnings she bought a building in downtown Manhattan that now houses a bank. She raised two beautiful daughters in New York City and eventually bought a beautifully decorated apartment in Manhattan. Her amazing fairy-tale story, which she peppered with memories of her children and friends, captured my attention. Our life circumstances were so different, but our adventurous soul personalities were so very similar.

As we talked, however, her dark eyes seemed to grow suddenly darker. "You know, no matter what I did or how much I accomplished, I felt like I was a disappointment to my mama. When I was a little girl, she always said, 'You are so self-centered. You get so distracted and never think of others. You are selfish.'"

Tears filled my friend's eyes as she continued. "I remember my mama's disappointment in me from the time I was about eight years old, and it has followed me my whole life. Before she died last year, I wish—just once—that she would have blessed me and told me she liked who I was. But instead, I'm left with her voice whispering to me of my inadequacy. I think I'll always carry some guilt because of that, as well as the 'brand' of being selfish."

Her story cut to the deepest places of my own heart. My new friend was lovely, friendly, competent, thoughtful, and spiritually hungry. Yet despite all of her accomplishments, she was still influenced by the voice she carried in her head.

Identify the Negative Voices

My own story is similar in many ways to that of my new friend. I wasted many years thinking that if I just tried a little harder or accomplished a little more, I would someday be acceptable to those who had criticized me as I was growing up.

I never tried to be a dreamer-idealist; that's just how I came out of the womb. I loved embarking on adventures, meeting people, taking risks, and challenging the "accepted" paths of life. Yet my dancing, singing, laughing soul seemed to irritate my family. I was left feeling as if I was "too much," or somehow wrong, for most people.

I wasted years thinking that if I just tried a little harder or accomplished a little more, I would be acceptable to those who had criticized me.

Sometimes the criticism was spoken; more often it was unspoken, though it cut just as deeply. How do you come up with all those weird ideas? You just try to be different to embarrass us. By the way, how are you doing on your weight? Have you been keeping your hair pretty? You know your looks matter so much—and blondes have to try harder in life because they have no natural coloring with those white eyelashes and colorless eyebrows.

These assessments may seem irrational now, but they devastated me when I was younger. I lived under the shadow of never feeling that I quite measured up—knowing that I was sure to disappoint no matter how hard I tried to be a "good, conforming little girl."

Sometimes the negative voices in our minds are part of the fallout of bad decisions—either our own or those of other people. These internal critics may point fingers of accusation at our hearts and paralyze us from moving through life with freedom and emotional health. I know so many women who lug around the dark places of their past and live under the burden of condemnation.

Weighty scars might lurk in hidden dark corners: abortion, immorality, sexual or physical abuse, divorce, an eating disorder, drug addiction, abandonment by parents, and more. As a result, the mental picture women have of themselves may be marred by inadequacy, guilt, insecurity, and self-criticism. And some of us are plagued by our tendency toward gossip, complaining, anger, bitterness, passivity, or disbelief. If we allow ourselves to fall into these bad habits, the internal voices they stir up will drain any energy and joy from our lives.

Add to that the ridiculous voices of culture that arbitrarily define beauty, success, and accomplishment, convincing us that we have to be a certain size, weight, and muscle mass. Advertising, commercials, and infomercials, as well as Facebook and blogs, stir our desire to become more acceptable, promise ways to make us belong, and suggest the formula for living well and "doing life right." Of course, they then generally lead us, the consumers, in the direction of a product for sale. Listening to such marketing schemes is a dead-end endeavor, yet I meet few women who have learned to ignore these voices entirely.

Christian communities add to the weight of guilt we carry. We know we should feed the hungry, adopt orphans, rescue young prostitutes, take short-term mission trips, give to the homeless, share Christ with our neighbors, worship in a certain way, have astounding experiences with God, submit in marriage, teach a Bible study, volunteer for the nursery, host an international student in our homes, mother our children and teach them the Bible . . . and that's just a partial list!

Then we're given formulas postulated for a perfect marriage, the ten rules on disciplining children, and the seven spiritual principles that will make us happy. Often the very works we are supposed to do keep us feeling distant from the God who longs to be close to us. If we can't check off all the boxes, we never feel as if we measure up. No wonder we subconsciously feel guilty and as if we are accomplishing so little for God.

These voices of secular and Christian culture shout at us through the media every day. Add to them the voices of childhood that produce lifelong scars, and most women come up feeling short of the mark they are supposed to reach. Only God offers deep-down inner acceptance and approval. Only His unconditional love and acceptance will satisfy our longings. Only His ways bring vibrant health.

Paul confronted the same issues in Galatia, where people saved by grace were being told to live by the law. He responded, "It was for freedom that Christ set us free; therefore keep standing firm and do not be subject again to a yoke of slavery" (Galatians 5:1).

Finding Freedom When We Feel We're Falling Short

We all carry internal voices that accuse us of inadequacy, that insist our failures must define us, and that assure us we will never live up to the arbitrary standards of others. Christian, the hero in John Bunyan's *Pilgrim's Progress*, is pictured dragging along through much of life because of the huge weighty burden he carries on his back. I frequently meet women, many of whom are Christ followers, who also carry baggage. They have lugged it around for so long that they do not even recognize how burdensome it is and how much energy it steals from their lives.

Until we identify the burdens we carry, the voices we have become accustomed to hearing in our heads, and the fingers that accuse us about past sins, we cannot move forward. Whatever the sources of our burdens, we do not have to carry them. We are quite free to accept the newness and freshness of life that Jesus granted. No matter what we have done or what we will do, we are not defined by our earthly lives, but by the healing, redeeming life of Jesus and His heavenly Father.

Maybe you're thinking, *Well, Sally, I'm actually feeling pretty good about myself right now.* This is truly the place where God wants you and me to live—so if you do not struggle with your self-image in this way, you are moving forward in maturity. This is an essential component of a vibrant spiritual life—to decide to like who we are because God loves us as we are.

I receive hundreds if not thousands of letters each year from women who feel inadequate or live under a burden of performance where they assume they always fall short of the expectations of God and others. They think, *I did fail. I should have stuck to my diet! I have no self-control.* Or, *Why did I just say that? My mother was right—I'm always sticking my foot in my mouth, and that will never change!*

Owning your life must begin with a healthy view of yourself that is based on what God thinks of you.

While we might succeed at "positive self-motivation" temporarily, when our self-perception is tied to our own accomplishments or others' evaluations, we will inevitably sink back into disappointment. Experiencing lasting newness of life requires a heart action on our part—engaging our wills and thoughts with the promises of God and the truth of Scripture.

Owning your life—your actions and decisions, and their consequences—must begin with a healthy view of yourself that is based on what God thinks of you. Once you listen to His voice, your self-perception will change. Whereas the negative voices lead only to guilt, inadequacy, fear, and discouragement, God wants to draw you forward to new possibilities, creativity, hope, inspiration, and courage. How I wish I had learned at an earlier age not to define myself by what other people thought of me.

Proverbs 29:25 (NLT) reminds us that "fearing people is a dangerous trap, but trusting the LORD means safety." Placing your confidence in the approval of someone else's validation provides a false hope that will always disappoint. Trying to live up to all the voices around you in this world will always leave you feeling inadequate.

Accepting our limitations and the inadequacies of others is key to freeing ourselves from self-condemnation. The reality is, we can all grow, but we will never change completely until we are in heaven. Choosing to be content and learning to be joyful is part of the process of becoming a new person. God is a champion for us. His desire is that we grow in our appreciation of just what it meant for Him to pay for all of our sins and make us new creatures so that we can become mature adults who live free from unnecessary guilt or unreasonable expectations.

Over time, I learned biblical secrets that led me to like myself, live free from guilt, enjoy my uniqueness, and even learn how to turn off the barrage of voices that tempt me to feel inadequate.

Learning to Like Yourself

In our world, physical attractiveness seems to count for a great deal, so it can be difficult to get past cultural standards of beauty. Yet you don't have to get stuck here. I once read, "French women are beautiful because they think they are beautiful." In other words, what we think often determines who we are.

In the 1995 movie version of *A Little Princess*, a young girl who had been born into a life of privilege is reduced to becoming a poor, bedraggled housemaid when it appears that her father has lost all his wealth and left her penniless. Now she must work as a servant to other wealthy girls at a private school, where the matron constantly condescends to her. The little girl's response to the harsh remarks of this small-souled matron is a defining quotation for all women: "I am a princess. All girls are. Even if they live in tiny old attics. Even if they dress in rags, even if they aren't pretty, or smart, or young. They're still princesses."[1]

From God's point of view, you, too, are a princess. After all, He is a king, and if you've chosen to follow Him, He has adopted you as His daughter. Your past is wiped away, and your future is defined by His adoption of you.

Deciding to like yourself is a choice to validate God's design on your life. Squandering your days wishing you were different is a waste of time. You have an ability to sparkle as you are in ways that no one else will ever be able to match. That's because self-acceptance will give you divine energy to live into the potential of the distinctive personality, body, mind, and circumstances that uniquely define the parameters of your life. God's desire is for you to love yourself as you are. Truly, you are a designer model, made to be one of a kind.

We would never tell a zebra that its stripes should have been polka dots, or a buffalo that it should flit around as delicately as a butterfly. And yet the world tries to fit us into a common mold, which leaves 99.9 percent of us feeling that we fall short compared to the imaginary standard of beauty and womanhood.

Women often tell me they will be happy "when I lose ten pounds" or "if we could just get another job and make more money" or "if my children were like your children." Or, or, or . . . the illusion that we'll be happier or more satisfied with life once something happens is a lie. Self-acceptance will be elusive until we decide to be content with who we are, warts and all. The psalmist reminds us,

> You made all the delicate, inner parts of my body
> and knit me together in my mother's womb.
> Thank you for making me so wonderfully complex!
> Your workmanship is marvelous—how well I know it.
> PSALM 139:13-14, NLT

When I affirm that I am a creation of God's hands, given significance by His own design, I move toward loving who He has created me to be.

Never will you be acceptable to every single person you meet. The same core sin nature that makes children fuss over who will get the toy also leads to petty fights in marriage, creates rifts among friends, and causes churches to split—and it resides in every person you will ever meet. (And must I add, *you* will also not be fair or loving to all the people who come into your life, right?) Until we get to heaven, every one of us must battle immaturity, prejudice, selfishness, and insecurity. Understanding that will keep you from allowing the negative attitudes that come your way to drag you down.

Over the years, I've received criticism on Facebook and in blog comments, as well as from friends, family, publishers, and other Christians. (I have always told my children that if they take a leadership role anywhere, they will be subject to criticism. Whenever they stand in front of people, they become an easier target. It is a necessary piece of wisdom to tuck away.) I may get twenty great responses to one of my blog articles or twenty great reviews of my book on Amazon. But often, if just one person leaves a negative comment or writes a negative review, I am tempted to carry the negative comment in my heart and allow it to hurt me in deep, insecure places.

I do not have the power to make everyone like me or approve of my values, looks, actions, or performance. But I am responsible for how I react to others' criticism of me. If I allow their words to destroy my self-image, then I am allowing them to control me. As I have grown in my walk with God, I've thankfully realized that allowing others to control the way I think about myself is a dark, endless hole. I am committed to gradually growing and learning in every area of my life, but essentially I have accepted that I will always be the same person under it all. I must daily decide to enjoy the person God made me to be.

In many ways, this has freed me to become more childlike, even as I grow older. I am freer to laugh, have fun, enjoy life, and celebrate the minutes because I care less about what others think as I live into the new person that I am in Christ.

Live in the Grace of Your New Self

As I awakened one gloriously warm, flowers-budding, birds-singing day, I breathed in the freshness. I walked down the stairs toward my first cup of brew thinking, *Today, I am going to have a good day. I will not sin with my mouth; I will not have a bad attitude; I will rule the day accordingly!*

As I sauntered into the kitchen, my younger daughter, Joy, smiled and asked, "What are you so chipper about?"

I told her, "I am in such a good mood today that I've decided I am not going to sin with my mouth even once today. I won't complain, be critical, or say something I will regret."

Laughing, she said, "Oh, Mama! Give it up. That is an unreasonable expectation!"

She was so right! I am surprised every day at my own propensity toward selfishness, immaturity, and sudden frustration or anger. I find all sorts of ways to sin! I make big and little mistakes even though I mean to be "good." Setting a standard of performance for myself that Jesus knows I cannot keep is a sure way to carry guilt.

Again, Scripture comes to mind. Romans 8:1 reminds us, "There is now no condemnation for those who are in Christ Jesus." If Jesus does not condemn you and me, then we should not allow the condemnation of other people or even the voices inside our heads to influence how we see ourselves.

This also applies to past sin, past flaws, past wickedness. Nothing we have ever done in the past and nothing we will ever do in the future can change the way God sees us. He sees you as righteous because of the work of His Son. When you accept Christ as your Savior, you also accept that as a new creature, you are completely acceptable as you are. "If anyone is in Christ, he is a new creature; the old things passed away; behold, new things have come" (2 Corinthians 5:17).

Daily, even moment by moment, when any feeling of insecurity, inadequacy, or failure wells up, you can go back to this truth. You can remind yourself, *I am a new creation, and all of my old nature and weaknesses passed away when I first loved Jesus.*

The process of growing a stronger self-image is not a one-time action, but it is a progressive strength. The more we practice thinking about God's unconditional love and acceptance, the easier it is to blow off the critics.

Owning our self-image is a work of grace that leads to the beauty of true womanhood. It is essential to becoming healthy and strong. And it begins when we allow God's voice of love to determine the state of our hearts.

✳

Own Your Part

Once when I was a young woman, my next-door neighbor said, "Sally, you are so very poised and gracious. What an amazing young woman you are!" Even though I did not know her well, I received words of affirmation so seldom that her words have stayed with me all of my life. They gave me a picture to live into. Because of the words she spoke into my life, I wanted to be poised and gracious.

There are many passages in Scripture that tell us of God's divine love. For example,

> The Lord appeared to him from afar, saying,
> "I have loved you with an everlasting love;
> Therefore I have drawn you with lovingkindness."
> JEREMIAH 31:3

1. If God loves you forever, then how can you receive this love into your heart and allow it to renew a healthy self-image?

   Write down in a journal or on a piece of paper the negative voices you listen to that accuse you or allow you to feel guilty or inadequate. Now write the verse above at the bottom of the page and remember that what God thinks about you is the truest thing about you.

2. Romans 8:1 says, "There is now no condemnation for those who are in Christ Jesus." When we accept His forgiveness by faith, we are able to live free from the feeling that somehow we are disappointing to Him. Identify the ways you feel you have fallen short

of His desires for you. Then memorize Romans 8:1 and bring it to your mind every time you are tempted to feel guilty.

3. Paul says in 2 Corinthians, "Anyone who belongs to Christ has become a new person. The old life is gone; a new life has begun!" (5:17, NLT).

    Remember that each day you live is a new day in which Jesus sees you as redeemed, forgiven, beloved, and innocent before His throne. At the beginning of each day, spend at least a couple of minutes acknowledging the newness of life that He provides you. Ask Him to usher you through each minute of your day and to keep His love present in your mind.

Praying with You

Heavenly Father, so often our ears are tuned to the voices that insist we are hopeless, guilty, and worthless. Please help us turn back to the truth of Your Word, which reminds us that we are redeemed, forgiven, and cherished. We thank You for demonstrating Your great love and compassion by sending Your Son to carry the weight of our sin. May our lives reflect the joy and freedom that are ours in Christ so that everyone we meet will be drawn to You, too. In Jesus' name, amen.

PART 2

Owning Your Vision

Mapping Your Life Purpose

CHAPTER 4

LIVING WITH THE END IN MIND

Owning Your Life Vision

A rock pile ceases to be a rock pile the moment a single man contemplates it, bearing within him the image of a cathedral.   ANTOINE DE SAINT-EXUPÉRY

LORD, remind me how brief my time on earth will be.
    Remind me that my days are numbered—
    how fleeting my life is.   PSALM 39:4, NLT

TWELVE OF MY DEAREST FRIENDS from Colorado Springs and I sat close together on my friend's covered back porch, sipping strong cups of English tea. We were enjoying the flowers from her gardens that graced the tables, the candles fluttering in the gentle wind, and the music playing softly in the background. I was savoring memories of many years shared together. Breathing in the late summer morning air, we all knew that the fall chill was tromping closely behind this glorious day. For a time, we simply enjoyed watching the aspen leaves dancing in the nearby trees like little girls twirling in the wind.

Finally, Phyllis, the hostess of this gathering, turned to me and said, "Dearest Sally, 'you is kind, you is smart, you is important'"—just like Aibileen told the little girl in the film *The Help*. "I mean that, sweet friend. And *you have changed your world*. I wonder how God will use you in the next twenty years of life to shine more of His light and beauty."

Tears sprang to my eyes, which surprised me. I didn't even know I needed to hear these words, but they comforted a deep place in my heart. As we diligently go through each day, plodding as faithfully as we can, holding together the cares of the world that seem to rest on our shoulders, we don't even know we need to hear "Well done!"

Yet the reason her affirmation meant so much was that she was a friend whom I admired because she had invested her life so intentionally to bring Christ's love to others. And so her affirmation of my life meant she could see the same in me.

My friend, Phyllis, had worked in Communist Eastern Europe at the same time I had. Even though she knew me well—my strengths and weaknesses—she recognized me as a fellow laborer for the cause of Christ, and that is why her validation meant so much. Both of us had invested our lives for Christ and His Kingdom.

As I reflected on her words, I was reminded anew that someday all of us will be in the presence of Jesus—the One who knows us better than any human ever could. Our lives, our choices, and our actions will testify to the legacy we left in this life. We will strain to hear Christ tell us, "Well done, . . . enter into the joy of your master" (Matthew 25:21), because His affirmation and validation are what each of us was created to enjoy.

Developing Personal Vision

The dreams inside point to the destiny each of us was created to fulfill. We each want to know that our lives matter and that we are not invisible. In the previous chapters, we talked about some of the self-imposed barriers that keep us from taking ownership of our lives. When we see them only as a series of mundane days, and when we become consumed by busyness and the nonstop media around us, our lives will become empty. When we focus on the expectations of others or dwell on the hurts they have caused us, we become prisoners to the circumstances of our lives. Ignoring the eternal purposes God has designed for us leads to emptiness.

When we fall into any of these traps, we tend to make excuses for the disappointment of living mundane, purposeless lives:

"I just don't have time for ministry to others."

"That sacrificial decision would not be financially feasible."

"I meant to write her a note [or call her when she was ill, or reach out to her when she was lonely, or give her some money when she was destitute], but it is too late now. I would probably just bother her."

"What would people think of me if I became that radical?"

"I might fail or embarrass myself."

"Why should I speak up? No one ever listens to me anyway."

Another extreme is when women try to control life and in essence try to control God, seeking to tame and manipulate their circumstances as much as possible in an attempt to avoid more stress and disappointment in life. In both cases, one year fades into another, each more disappointing than the last. If we are not careful, the sands of our lives will slip away, and our excuses will leave only empty echoes in the wind. Or as Henry David Thoreau noted, "The mass of men lead lives of quiet desperation."

As a little girl, Katie often covered her head with a pillow to drown out the shouts of her parents arguing in their bedroom. The initial relief she felt when they divorced quickly turned into a deep ache as her father's absence from school events and softball games left her feeling empty. She had no control over her parents' relationship, and now she continues to live like a victim who has no power to influence the destiny of her own life. Consequently, as a mother, she seeks to keep her children from all things difficult and to spare them any unhappiness. So ultimately she controls their days and lives but prevents them from developing

The dreams inside us point to the destiny we were created to fulfill.

the "spiritual muscle" they will need as adults to be able to flourish in the world.

Elizabeth happily married her high school sweetheart, but after having three children in five years, she often feels like an emotionless zombie, trudging through a life that seems to follow an endless cycle of "change diapers, make a meal, pick up toys, repeat." She feels void of happiness or joy and often wonders why God seems so passive, so far away. She longs for purpose and meaning beyond the drudgery of her life and wastes her days dreaming of some elusive day in the future when she thinks she will be happy again.

Joanie married after graduate school and hoped that her husband would meet the deep emotional needs of her life. But after several years, she found out that he was addicted to pornography and had multiple affairs while he was on the road for work. As a single woman again, divorced, she lives in fear of trusting others or God with her future.

All of these precious women stuff their feelings, afraid to look into their souls or at the consequences of their choices and behavior, wondering if the hopelessness is their own fault, moving through one day after another without change and without hope for something better. There are so many other scenarios of women who tell me they feel empty, lonely, unseen. Yet it seems that each of these women has lost or never had a vision for the immense value of the days granted her by the Lord and the significance of every single day—even amidst some brokenness. The truth is, all of us live in the tension of brokenness and the hope of an eternity when all will be whole.

Jesus told a story that has captivated my imagination and won't let go because it deals with this very heart attitude. Many of us are familiar with the parable of the talents in Matthew 25, in which a master entrusted part of his wealth to three of his servants before he left on a journey. The first was given five talents; the second, two; and the third, one—each according to his individual ability.

The first two were good stewards who made a profit on the talents they'd been given. The third servant, Jesus said, "dug a hole in the ground and hid the master's money" (verse 18, NLT).

When the master returned home, he called his servants in individually to report on how they'd invested what he'd given them. The first two servants had doubled their talents. The pleased master told each of them, "Well done, my good and faithful servant. You have been faithful in handling this small amount, so now I will give you many more responsibilities. Let's celebrate together!" (verses 21 and 23).

The third servant was then called in to explain how he'd used his one talent. Listen to his excuse: "Master, I knew you were a harsh man, harvesting crops you didn't plant and gathering crops you didn't cultivate. I was afraid I would lose your money, so I hid it in the earth. Look, here is your money back" (verses 24-25).

The master responded, "You wicked and lazy servant! . . . Why didn't you deposit my money in the bank? At least I could have gotten some interest on it" (verses 26-27).

Jesus concluded, "To those who use well what they are given, even more will be given, and they will have an abundance. But from those who do nothing, even what little they have will be taken away" (verse 29). Jesus, who forgave prostitutes and cheating tax collectors, refers to this third servant as a wicked, lazy man. I can think of only a couple of times in the Gospels when Jesus spoke harshly. In the other instances, He was speaking to or about the Pharisees, those law-driven and rule-keeping religious leaders who lacked compassion and didn't acknowledge that Jesus was the Son of God. He certainly condemns this third servant as well.

There seems to be no place for passivity and indifference in our walk with God. That, I believe, is particularly incriminating to our generation of Christians. Yet Jesus is not an exacting or unreasonable, demanding God. Throughout Scripture, we see that He is:

patient with our sins: "There is now no condemnation for those who are in Christ Jesus." (Romans 8:1) faithful to train and lead us step-by-step to maturity: "He who began a good work in you will perfect it until the day of Christ Jesus." (Philippians 1:6)

compassionate: "The LORD is . . . slow to anger and abounding in lovingkindness." (Psalm 103:8)

Nonetheless, once we belong to Jesus, we are the stewards of His good gifts. A heart that lacks the will to grow or invest for the Kingdom of God is evidently a wicked heart to the master in the story, or in reality, to Jesus. He has given each of us, according to our gifts and circumstances, a "talent" to use well. If we do not invest ourselves spiritually, we will incur His anger when we stand before Him someday. It does not matter whether we bury the opportunities He has given us out of passivity, indifference, fear, procrastination, or anger. Like the third servant, our excuses will fall flat.

God loves us and desires us to respond to Him. So while He is utterly compassionate, He is looking for hearts that seek to obey and trust Him:

Without faith it is impossible to please Him.

HEBREWS 11:6

Even so faith, if it has no works, is dead, being by itself.

JAMES 2:17

During our lifetimes, each of us has incredible potential to be a powerful influence for righteousness, love, goodness, compassion, mercy, and redemption—and to find joy and contentment in each day. Yet how willing we are to work toward pleasing our Master determines the destiny of our lives.

God gave each of us a will—the ability to decide what we are "willing" to do. He did not make us like puppets that can be forced to act in a certain way. Instead, He created us so that we must set the direction of our own hearts and minds. Our attitudes ultimately guide our moment-by-moment choices, as well as the biggest decisions of our lives.

Our spiritual vision can be defined by the way each of us sees our interior self, as well as our purpose and stewardship here on earth. Put another way, each of us has been offered a part in the drama of mankind—God's mega-story, the way Christ is redeeming all things to Himself. Yet to play our part in the overarching narrative, we must understand the role we have been uniquely created to perform. We've been given distinct personalities, circumstances, capacities, and potential to invest and from which to craft a life of excellence.

God considers us to be sacred, holy vessels. The words *sacred* and *holy* infer that we are singularly designed and intrinsically valuable to God. He invites us to "come out and be separate"[2] from the ways of the world. We are called to become dedicated warriors, so to speak, for His side and to battle for His Kingdom throughout this world. Unlike the third servant, we should not be passive or terrified by that responsibility. He has not left us alone, but desires to empower our hearts, minds, and souls by giving us His Spirit to live inside us.

If you dedicate yourself to taking in spiritual wisdom from Scripture, giving yourself wholly to the purposes of God, disciplining the attitudes of your heart, and stepping out in faith to show Jesus to the world, God will use you to shape history for His glory.

Becoming a World Changer Requires Your Will

Psychologists suggest that all people have the intrinsic desire and drive to live up to their potential and to do something significant with their lives. They call this process self-actualization.

Many people today lack spiritual self-actualization—the realization that God created them with the intrinsic potential of living significant, powerful, influential lives. While we live supernatural lives only through the power of the Spirit of God, we must choose to take the necessary risks to live spiritually powerful lives.

Perhaps you feel that is too lofty a goal for someone as ordinary as you. If so, consider the earthly life of Jesus. The One who formed the galaxies in our universe, who crafted the waterfalls, and who can contain a tornado could have chosen to make Himself known to the world in some uniquely powerful way. He could have entered the world through a lightning storm or a star falling from the sky. And yet He came to earth as a dependent, vulnerable baby—just like each one of us did. He learned the Shema, or the law of God, in the small village where His parents, a carpenter and a common Jewish girl, raised Him. His family lived in a country in which Roman soldiers oppressed and demeaned the Jewish faith. They were subject to inordinate taxes, and they had to work hard to feed their family. You cannot find a much humbler setting than the one into which our Savior was born.

Recently, I was reminded that a normal life can have extraordinary results even today. Many years ago, a young couple went through a contentious divorce and ended up battling for custody of their children. Their family was not only being split apart; the little ones were also publicly questioned in court and sent from one household to another until the question of custody was ultimately decided.

My elderly friend knew this family from church. Though she did not have the energy she once had to care for small children, she was convinced that God wanted her to invite the two children to spend their spring break in her home. To welcome them, she baked cookies and cupcakes that had been her own children's favorites. She also cooked a pot roast and placed balloons at the front door.

Grasping his favorite book, *Green Eggs and Ham*, under his arm, the little boy slowly followed his sister into my friend's home. With wide eyes, he said, "This is just like walking into a Christmas house. It is so beautiful with all the balloons and cupcakes!"

Throughout the week, my friend read *Green Eggs and Ham* over and over to the little boy. "I like it when someone reads this to me 'cause my mama and daddy gave it to me the last time we had Christmas together," he told her. Saying "Sam-I-am" became a ritual they shared before breakfast and each good-night kiss.

The boy was especially fearful at bedtime. When he was unable to go to sleep or when a nightmare woke him up, my friend would lay the little boy on her chest and rock him back and forth while singing "Jesus loves me, this I know. . . ."

The night before he and his sister headed home, the little boy's blue eyes glistened from the tears falling down his freckled face. Looking up at the kind elderly woman, he told her, "I think Jesus must look just like you, because when I am with you, I see Him all over you."

For years, she wrote those two children notes. She made them birthday cakes, and she prayed for them regularly. I learned all these details thirty years later when I met the little boy, now grown up, shortly after my friend had died. "I think she was one of the most influential people in my young life," he told me.

Jesus has chosen you to be a picture of Him to your world too. He loved you so you could share His love with everyone you meet. He forgave you so that you could extend grace to those who need to experience the forgiveness of a real, flesh-covered person. He lavished your world with beauty so you could reflect His beauty to those in your life. You may be the only Christ follower with access to your neighbors or coworkers. Every one of them needs Jesus, and they need to see His reality through you.

When you choose to invest your life for His purposes, you are joining a host of faithful followers down through the centuries. When He was on earth, Jesus chose ordinary people to be His followers and then lead His Kingdom movement—fishermen, tax collectors, prostitutes. Apart from His twelve disciples, His closest friends were Lazarus and his two sisters—Martha, a willing hostess, and Mary, who seemed more interested in listening to Jesus than in serving food.

These common folk took Jesus at His word. Even the religious leaders recognized the power of God in the lives of these ordinary people: "The members of the council were amazed when they saw the boldness of Peter and John, for they could see that they were ordinary men with no special training in the Scriptures. They also recognized them as men who had been with Jesus" (Acts 4:13, NLT).

God desires to work supernaturally through normal people who are willing to follow Him wholeheartedly and reflect His glory. Christianity is not just about giving on Sunday, yawning through church, or providing a special offering once in a while to the poor. God's exceptional call on our lives may seem extreme to most people.

God desires to work supernaturally through normal people who are willing to follow Him wholeheartedly and to reflect His glory.

Yet the folly of believers has always been to trifle life away and ignore His calling.

But when Christ gets ahold of one's life and the Holy Spirit lives through an ordinary person like you or me, the redeeming power of God bubbles over and touches every aspect of life. To drive this point home to my children, I often repeated this mantra as they were growing up: "It is natural to quarrel, to be selfish, to live a small-minded life. It is supernatural to love unconditionally, to serve others, to live a life of vision and faith." Choose to live a supernatural life!

In our own flesh, we face limitations. No matter how much we would love to become excellent, we will sometimes fail in our attempts to be unselfish. Yet Jesus came to provide grace for us in every task.

In my quest to live for His Kingdom, I trust in His ability to do great things. I yield my days to Him, believing that He will be faithful to work through me, that He will take my paltry fish and loaves, as He did with the little boy. As I offer Him all that I have, I will accomplish more in His Spirit than I could ever have done by myself. I yield my burdens to Him, knowing that He will show up because He is my dependable Father.

How Will You Invest Your Life?

Such thoughts went through my mind that morning as I sat on the deck sipping tea with my friends at my birthday breakfast. I considered how God had worked through our lives. Though my friends and

I had worked in different Christian ministries and different countries, we had undergone similar experiences. We were not uniquely educated or gifted people, but we had been challenged by life-changing messages that shaped the decisions and courses of our lives. As young women we had heard over and over again that we had only one life to invest for the Kingdom of God and that God wanted to work through us to change the world. We knew that "we are His workmanship, created in Christ Jesus for good works, which God prepared beforehand so that we would walk in them" (Ephesians 2:10). We took Him at His word, obeying and following Him wherever He led—and so we became world changers as we followed Him to the ends of the earth.

Determining what good works He created for you to do is essential to understanding how God might use you. Unless you evaluate your life, count the cost of serving God, and make a plan for how you will move ahead, reading this book will be of no help.

For years, my husband and I have reviewed the plans we have made at least once a year, and sometimes every six months. As a matter of fact, I recently took a few days away to decide what kind of woman I want to be in the next ten years and what ministry God is working to build into my heart during this season. I then made a plan of how to practically move forward toward these goals, which included pulling out of some current commitments so I might follow the paths God is directing me to follow during this time of my life.

Own Your Part

Young though she was, my friend Judy had lived through the divorce of her parents, her mother's alcoholism, and sexual abuse from an uncle that she was afraid to reveal to her busy parents. Yet in college, someone shared Christ with her, and for the first time, she found the love, forgiveness, and hope she had always longed to experience. She studied the Bible every day and asked to be mentored by a woman she had met. As the years passed, she cultivated great compassion for others with broken pasts, so she began to write short devotionals for women on a personal blog and started small groups for young women in her home. She felt so fully redeemed that she made her story a means of offering compassion, restoration, and healing for others who longed to know Christ's love.

You, too, have a story worth telling, an opportunity to bring the light of Christ into your world, right where you are. It is my prayer that as you seek to take ownership of your life, you will be renewed, refreshed, and inspired to live into the wonderful life God has created for you to embrace.

1. As you place your dreams, plans, and stewardship of your life into His hands, you will hear Him whispering ideas to pursue, sins to confess, areas to strengthen, and people to reach. What dreams have you always had in your heart that He might want you to pursue? What messages are particularly meaningful to you, and how might you begin to share these with others?

2. Someday each of us will have to give an account to God for how we made His messages known in our world. How then might you specifically live into your heritage as a Christian? What are your skills? Your drives? Your talents that God might use for His glory? What do you feel is a special strength or skill that God has given you to use to encourage others—giving, serving, encouraging, writing, teaching, cooking, hospitality, mercy, compassion for the lost?

Often the story and circumstances of your life will influence your message. How do you want to use what you have experienced to speak into those who have similar lives? List three practical things you can do to begin serving those around you who need encouragement, help, or guidance.

Are you willing to live by faith and bring His influence to bear in every aspect of your life—to live each day filled with His love and power? When Jesus lives through someone, He always moves that person to do what is on His heart. He is always concerned to redeem others through the life that is yielded to Him.

3. If God lived fully through your life, what could He bring to pass?

4. Who in your life needs to know God's love and goodness?

5. How have you manifested and taught God's truth and values to people who long for wisdom and direction?

6. In the power of the Holy Spirit, what will you dream for His glory?

7. Can you think of any way He would want to use you to influence your world in your lifetime?

Praying with You
Heavenly Father, bless those who read this book. Show them the deep wellspring of Your love; give them the courage of faith that comes from knowing You, our great God; give them wisdom to figure out how to live their present lives in a way that brings harmony; and give them the companionship of Your Spirit each step of the way. Amen.

CHAPTER 5

LOOKING TO GOD AS YOUR LIFE COACH

Owning God's Training

This is all the inheritance I can give to my dear family; the religion of Christ can give them one which will make them rich indeed. PATRICK HENRY

You are a chosen race, a royal priesthood, a holy nation, a people for God's own possession, so that you may proclaim the excellencies of Him who has called you out of darkness into His marvelous light. 1 PETER 2:9

FROM THE TIME HE WAS A LITTLE BOY, my older son, Joel, always bubbled over with music, whether humming a song, strumming a guitar, or fiddling on a piano. Because our family moved seventeen times—including six international relocations—he picked up most of his knowledge on his own or in our home, where music was always playing, rather than through regular music lessons.

Even with little formal training, Joel was accepted into Berklee College of Music in Boston, one of the foremost contemporary music schools in the United States. His professors were outstanding musicians who held him to high standards. Because the school was quite expensive and money was tight in our family, Joel carried the stress of helping to provide for his expenses. He worked two jobs as he sought to finish his degree in composition within two and a half years. From the start, he had to follow a demanding schedule of ceaseless practicing, composing, and working.

In his final year, he also entered a composing competition, which made his grueling schedule even more overwhelming. One cold November day, Joel called home. I still remember the grave despair in his voice. "Mom, I need to talk to you. I feel like I am going to crash. I am constantly exhausted, and I have had the flu for two weeks. On top of that, I am working my two jobs, trying to do well in classes, and finishing my composition. It just feels like too much. I don't know if I can do all of this well. I feel like quitting. I really need some help."

As a mom, I felt conflicted. I knew Joel had been working incredibly hard, and I was concerned about his health. Since I'd been over-committed at various times in my life, I could understand Joel's feelings and felt compassion for him.

On the other hand, I wanted to help Joel finish the course God had given him if he was able to stick with it. As an older woman, I had come to understand that my capability to be strong and endure difficulties was always greater than I felt in moments of exhaustion or discouragement. I could look back and see that God had stretched me to show me that His capacity through me was more than I could ever have understood.

I knew that emotions often dictate our decisions when life becomes challenging. When that happens, we often quit. In fact, we live in an era of compromise, and we're often encouraged to take the easier route and give ourselves a break.

Yet when quitting becomes our default response to tough circumstances, we will never know the joy of finishing strong or hearing "well done" when we've finished a task. We also lose many prime opportunities for character training.

In fact, as I look back at my own life, I see that God expanded my abilities when I walked through seasons of having to press on. Owning and submitting to God's training process is essential to developing our inner character.

I talked sympathetically to my son as he shared his heart with me. "Joel, I can't even imagine how exhausted you must feel. You have been amazingly committed, and I know working so many hours and having to manage so much stress must be draining. Drop whatever you can for the next few days. Get some sleep, eat well, and then let's talk whenever you want. I will help you through this time."

Over the next several months, I was determined to be a voice of hope, encouragement, and help to Joel. I sought to boost his confidence and cheer him on as he juggled many important tasks. I made frequent calls and a weekend visit. I prayed with him and for him. I also sent him money so he could go out for meals. I sent a number of greeting cards, in which I penned many short notes that expressed my confidence in his abilities:

"God is with you and He will see you through."
"God has given you such incredible capacity, and I see you
      growing stronger every time you resolve to finish well! I am
      so proud of your diligence and strength of character!"
"I will help you in any way I can. You are doing such a
      great job."

My commitment to Joel was sure. He was my beloved first son. All his life I had joyfully dedicated myself to protecting him, helping him, loving him, and encouraging him. Because I delighted in him, I wanted to do whatever I could to help him succeed.

As his parent, I saw my role as helping him through his challenges, not removing them. I would do just about anything I could to help him complete the tasks he had been given. But Joel would have to do the work himself in order to achieve his goals—compose the music, practice, and show up at his jobs. He would have to lean into the process of character training that his life required.

Months after that initial phone conversation, he called me again. "I can't believe it, Mom! My composition has won the competition, and it will be performed with two other pieces here in Boston in the concert hall. The two other winners and I will receive honors as composers of the year that night too. You have to come with me to the concert, Mom. You were such a part of helping me get through these last months."

My younger daughter, Joy, flew with me to Boston. On the night of the concert, we dressed up in traditional black formal attire and headed to the concert hall. As we walked to our seats up front, Joel whispered to me nervously, "I think they were just being nice to me when they picked my composition. Hope you are not disappointed." I squeezed his arm and gave him a reassuring smile. As a public speaker, I knew the anxiety and self-doubt that creep in when you're about to bare your ideas—or music—to a crowd of people you don't know.

A few minutes later, a professional pianist strode onstage to play Joel's piece. As his hands danced among the keys, the musician hit crescendos and pianissimos and all sorts of trills in between. When he reached the end of Joel's piece, the audience jumped to their feet and gave my son a standing ovation. As they cheered enthusiastically, Joel stood up and smiled sheepishly. After the concert, many of his friends and teachers walked up to him to shake his hand or give him an exuberant slap on the back.

My delight in the joy of my son's deep satisfaction and happiness spilled to overflowing. Whether Joel had won or been applauded had not been my concern. I wanted to help him discover the strength he possessed by enduring this challenging year. I wanted to coach him so that he would recognize his own potential and see how deep his latent skill really was.

I knew his willingness to put forth great effort and endure discomfort had produced great fruit through the music he had created. In the process of straining toward his high goals, Joel had also stretched his faith and his capacity to work harder to develop the potential God had granted him. Yet this growth hadn't come automatically; he had to own it by his own intention. As a mother, I was thrilled to see the growth and freedom he experienced as a result of this success.

Indeed, when he returned home that summer, we agreed that he had been transformed from a young student into a full-fledged strong man of character. He had run the race, endured through exhaustion, and finished well. To quit before reaching the finish line deprives us of the reward of completion and the strengthening of our character.

It Is All Good

I now realize that, just as I had coached Joel because I wanted my son to become all he was created to be, so God walks beside each one of us, offering encouragement and giving us the strength we need to fulfill our individual potential. Like any parent, God wants His children to thrive and live with purpose. That is just one sense in which He made us like Himself. As we learn in the very first chapter of the Bible, "God created human beings in his own image. In the image of God he created them" (Genesis 1:27, NLT).

God walks beside each one of us, offering encouragement and giving us the strength we need to fulfill our potential.

Of course, even before God formed man from the dust of the ground and breathed the breath of life into his nostrils, He had prepared a place for His children to dwell. The Garden of Eden was a place of beauty, variety, color, sound, and pleasure. Its splendor reflected God's great esteem and value for His creatures. This Garden was to be the place where people would share God's vast life and glory, in companionship with Him.

After creating the Garden, God desired to craft a creature like Himself, who could live purposefully and fully thrive in living out his destiny. So God our Father blew the radiant breath of life into the very being of Adam. "The LORD God formed man of dust from the ground, and breathed into his nostrils the breath of life; and man became a living being" (Genesis 2:7).

God not only set Adam and Eve in a beautiful garden but also granted them the authority to:

make decisions of influence (to rule over the world and
    subdue it)

accomplish great feats of artistic design and discover the science
of His Creation (by giving them minds that could think and
process great and abstract thoughts)

know the depths of intimate love (by giving them the will and
emotions to connect to others)

write profound treatises of truth

This was to be our inheritance—to share in God's vast life and
glory in companionship with Him. And His very life, His Spirit, had
been breathed into man's being.

God designed man with the ability to accomplish great feats. Work
was a good creation, providing us with the pleasure of accomplishment and allowing us to find validation in expressing the glory of
God's mark on our lives.

Even as Joel had a dormant capacity to create music, he had to
tap into his potential and nurture the talent and apply his wisdom to
compose a beautiful piece of music. And so each of us has latent skills
and talents, hidden within and designed by God, that we must choose
to develop and nurture in our lifetimes.

God is with us to support us, just as I had helped Joel. He intends
us to find fulfillment in the work of life we were created to accomplish. It is our glory as God's people to be able to apply ourselves to
become productive, and God delights in our vigorous engagement of
life. As a good parent, God offers not just emotional love but also a
commitment to the development of our spiritual, emotional, physical,
and mental well-being.

Our pedigree, our heritage from the very beginning, from the
inception of Creation, was that we would be like this amazing and
loving God, our Father, who said, "Let Us make man in Our image,
according to Our likeness" (Genesis 1:26).

He crafted us to live fully as creative beings, agents of His own
capacity: to rule, subdue, and express our own imprint on the world,
filled with the life and scope of His Spirit, who lives within us.

Through our new birth—from death to life—we become ambassadors, light bearers, lovers, and architects of all things excellent. We become just like Him in our ability to live purposefully, intentionally, and authoritatively.

This is our history, and this is our inheritance. The very imprint of the fingertips of God rests mysteriously in the depths of our being.

And God pronounced that all He had made was good; and even better, when He created man, He said it was very good.

Thorns, Thistles, and Sweat

Even at the dawn of the creation of mankind, a snake was lurking in the Garden. Satan jealously regarded the glory and freedom God had given to man as something he wished to destroy. Longing for his own praise, he desired to own for himself the allegiance of the creature made in the image of God.

God had warned Adam, "From any tree of the garden you may eat freely; but from the tree of the knowledge of good and evil you shall not eat, for in the day that you eat from it you will surely die" (Genesis 2:16-17).

And yet, turning away from the very words and voice of God, Adam and Eve inclined their ears to the whispers of the world, to the very voice of Satan.

His desire to lie, deceive, and destroy motivated him to question God's integrity and intent: "The serpent said to the woman, 'You surely will not die! For God knows that in the day you eat from it your eyes will be opened, and you will be like God, knowing good and evil'" (Genesis 3:4-5).

From the beginning, temptation came from listening to the wisdom of the one who deceives. The deceptive voices of the world—lies, false promises, false security, soul destruction—have multiplied exponentially over the years.

Adam and Eve chose to listen to the serpent. Devastating, heartbreaking results incurred a curse on the whole world as a result. Adam and Eve did not die at that moment physically. What happened, then? God removed His Spirit from them—His breath-life, the beautiful design of God's purposes.

The same Spirit who had created life to be beautiful, righteous, and good now no longer lived in the soul of man. And so man became his own source of knowledge, purpose, and morality. In short, with the absence of God inside him, man was left to his own limited and corrupt perspective of how to live. Man has been living for himself and by his own faulty wisdom since the separation between God and man.

Taking Back the Lost Ground

The apostle Paul tells us that man continues to determine his own way of wisdom in life: "Even though they knew God, they did not honor Him as God or give thanks, but they became futile in their speculations, and their foolish heart was darkened. Professing to be wise, they became fools" (Romans 1:21-22).

What's the solution? Christian theologians often talk about sanctification, which is the process of becoming like Jesus—again! Plastic surgery provides a simple if incomplete illustration of what sanctification does to those souls who have been justified, or redeemed, by Christ. Just as plastic surgeons have the amazing capacity to transform deformity, obesity, and unwanted facial characteristics into something new and more beautiful, so God desires to remove the scars caused by our brokenness, to heal the deformity caused by sin, and to use the ugliness of life to transform us into the beautiful image of Christ we were originally made to bear.

Of course, in order for a surgeon to sculpt beauty from brokenness, the patient must go under the knife. Likewise, the writer of Hebrews describes the tool God uses to reshape us into His own reflection:

> God's discipline is always good for us, so that we might
> share in his holiness. No discipline is enjoyable while it
> is happening—it's painful! But afterward there will be a

peaceful harvest of right living for those who are trained
in this way.   HEBREWS 12:10-11, NLT

The word *discipline* in Greek has a wonderful meaning. It does not
refer to someone being punished for doing something wrong. Instead,
it carries the meaning of a father training, educating, and bringing up
a child in wisdom with an aim toward maturity.

Consequently, God's discipline is His means of coming alongside
us to educate us and to call out our innate potential for excellence so
that we might become righteous and holy. God had great plans in
mind when He created Adam and Eve. He renews those plans for us
as He redeems us. That is why He wants us to accept His training,
even when it seems difficult. He knows that ultimately His discipline
will yield the peaceful fruit of righteousness in our lives. Even as I
stood by Joel when he was under so much pressure to simultaneously
apply his composition skills, work hard in his classes, and toil long
hours at two jobs, so God stands with us each step of the way to help
us fulfill our potential.

God allows difficulty in our lives to strengthen our spiritual
muscles. He provides stretching opportunities so we might exercise
and apply wisdom. All the while, He wants to empower us through
His voice of encouragement and the
strength we need to take one more
step. He never leaves us alone.

God allows difficulty in our lives to strengthen our spiritual muscles.

Notice that the writer of Hebrews
admits that this process can seem dif-
ficult and sometimes grueling, but in the end, His goal is to ensure we
have the character of Christ and can live into our original inheritance
of reflecting His very image to the world.

God Is the Great Re-Creator

Jesus came to redeem what was lost—to restore us to our original
design—so that He might live in and through us. In John 10:10, Jesus

tells us that "the thief [Satan] comes only to steal and kill and destroy; I came that they may have life, and have it abundantly." Jesus died to pay the penalty for our spiritual death.

In his Gospel, the disciple John gives his account of how the resurrected Jesus began restoring what had been lost when mankind fell into sin. In John 20, we learn that on the first evening after Jesus' resurrection, His disciples sat cowering behind locked doors. Suddenly Jesus stood in the midst of them. John recalls, "Jesus said to them again, 'Peace be with you; as the Father has sent Me, I also send you.' And when He had said this, He breathed on them and said to them, 'Receive the Holy Spirit'" (John 20:21-22).

God had blown the breath of life into Adam in the first Garden; now, He restored these men to their original design by breathing the Spirit into them. They were renewed, indwelled, and filled to the very brim with the life of God.

Not long after that, seven of the disciples headed out for a night of fishing on the Sea of Galilee. At dawn, after catching nothing all night, they heard a voice from the shore: "Cast the net on the right-hand side of the boat" (John 21:6). The men obeyed and had to strain to pull the overflowing net into the boat. Knowing it was Jesus, Peter jumped out of the boat and swam to shore. As he did, he must have been thinking about one of his first encounters with the Lord. On that day, too, Jesus had told him where to throw his nets into the water after catching nothing the day before. The haul had been so large that Peter had to call for another boat. Now, when Peter reached the shore, he found the resurrected Christ preparing a tantalizing feast of fresh fish over an open campfire to satisfy the appetites of his closest friends.

Peter knew that the resurrected Christ, who had blown the breath-life of the Spirit of God into him, was also the source of the overflowing miracle. Jesus' initiation and authority, not Peter's own laborious efforts, had brought the abundant catch of a lifetime.

These stories hold great promise for us as well. With the strength, power, love, and authority of Jesus pulsing through us, we, too, can have abundant lives. Not our strenuous efforts, but His life generously provides all we need for flourishing lives of ministry.

When we accepted God's offer of salvation, the Holy Spirit came into our lives. He was given to us so we might have His wisdom, develop godly character, and experience the productive lives we were made for. Once we understand our history and our part in God's story, we begin to understand how we can take back ground lost at the Fall.

God grants us great freedom and privilege to act out our own part in the great drama of life on earth. If we continue to follow our own shortsighted ways or the ways and expectations of the world, we will never flourish or find tranquillity. Remember the young woman writer I met in New York City? She wanted someone to bring peace in the midst of her chaos. I believe she is seeking a dead end. To have the peace and blessing of God, we must intentionally identify and move away from the sources of chaos. Only then can we begin living consciously into God's design for our lives. Only then can we hear the quiet voice and stirrings of our ultimate Life Coach.

✳

Own Your Part

In an attempt to make her son "happy," a woman I know always made excuses for her son when he acted selfishly, insulted other children, or made immoral choices during his teen years. Instead of gently training and instructing him, she allowed this child to always get his own way. Consequently, when he left home, this young man was unable to cope with the difficulties he encountered at his university. His mom retrieved him, one more time, and brought him back home from college, blaming others for her son's failure to withstand the pressures of college.

Since then, her son has gone from job to job, has been married twice, and is now living at home again. The woman recently said to me, "I was avoiding immediate discipline and training in the life of my son but now have deeper disappointments to bear because I never wanted him to be unhappy. How I wish I had disciplined him so he could have become a confident, strong man."

1. God is not so concerned that we are always happy as He is committed to helping us become mature and learn to be content. Begin to ask God how He wants you to live out your role in the story of life He has granted you. How can you live truthfully, heroically, and faithfully in such a way that you will fulfill the very destiny for which you were born? Where must you be faithful? How will you redeem the dark places in your life? How will you leave a legacy of faith that will give courage to those who come after you? Where does God want to see you develop excellence of character?

2. Your life is significant and meaningful in light of God's overall purposes. How will you own your decisions so that you may fulfill your divine and providential calling?

Paul reminds us in Philippians 2:13 that God "is at work in you, both to will and to work for His good pleasure." It brings God joy to see His children flourish, just as I delighted in Joel's accomplishments. Even when the road looks hard, Christ is at your side to strengthen you and to give you hope and encouragement. In the end, however, He leaves it to you to decide whether you will live with diligence and endurance.

Praying with You
Heavenly Father, help us to trust Your ways in our lives. Difficulties can sometimes overwhelm us. Give us the grace to keep taking one step at a time, to respond to Your training, and to rest each day as You carry us through. In Jesus' name we come. Amen.

PART 3

Owning Your Life by Giving God Control

What Only He Can Do

CHAPTER 6

RESTING IN THE TRANSCENDENCE OF GOD

Owning the Mystery of His Supremacy

As long as you are proud you cannot know God. A proud man is always looking down on things and people: and, of course, as long as you are looking down you cannot see something that is above you.   C. S. LEWIS, *MERE CHRISTIANITY*

Humble yourselves under the mighty hand of God, that He may exalt you at the proper time.   1 PETER 5:6

GRAVEL PINGED THE SIDES OF OUR CAR as we wound our way up the narrow dirt road, the ominous shadows of mountains surrounding our car. Moving away from Colorado had been a difficult decision, but now we were on our way back to visit our beloved friends and former next-door neighbors in the Rockies for an outdoor cookout. As I looked over my shoulder, thousands of city lights sparkled in the distance below. Glancing above, I saw thousands of stars in the navy sky, and my heart was filled with wonder. I realized that, although those stars have been up there since God threw them across the sky at the beginning of time, the city lights—fueled by bulbs that will someday burn out—obscure the infinite heavens.

I temporarily forgot the God-created light show as my family joined our friends for a feast of grilled steak, roasted herbed red potatoes, and fresh Colorado peaches topped with whipped cream. Afterward, the fifteen of us—chilled by the nighttime mountain air—snuggled together on patio couches and deck chairs, giggling as we squished together under rough wool blankets. Then our host, Danny, brought a high-powered telescope out to the patio. We became treasure hunters, sweeping our eyes across the sky as we searched for shooting stars. Far away from city lights, an infinite number of diamond sparkles were strewn before us, looking as if they'd been dramatically laid out against a navy velvet backdrop.

My children each took a turn at the telescope, gasping and wiggling in delight at all the marvels they could see. Afterward, they called out to me, "Mom, you have to see this—this is your star—it is bright blue!" They knew precisely which shade was my favorite color.

I peered into the scope, and it took my eyes a few seconds to adjust to the picture inside the long tube. When they did, I was unprepared for the magnificent sight. I had no idea how deeply beguiled my soul would be from viewing the intricate artistry of God among the constellations, cast out infinitely in the heavens above.

All my life, I had heard of "twinkling" stars, but I'd never seen one glimmering, shimmering, and sparkling so clearly. The astonishingly bright azure-blue star seemed to be dancing as it twinkled and turned elegantly in the sky. It almost took my breath away. Captivated by the beauty and elegance of its splendor, I wondered at the One who had created such beauty, knowing this bit of handiwork would be unobserved by the vast majority of people throughout the ages. Still, the luminous star sparkled vibrantly as though it couldn't repress offering a refrain of worship to the Artist who had crafted it.

I thought of the question God asked Job after Job had poured out his complaints. God challenged this righteous man to expand his perspective, reminding him that as the foundations of the earth were laid, the stars sang and a choir of heavenly hosts filled every crevice of the universe with praise. "Where were you . . ." God asked Job, "when the morning stars sang together and all the sons of God shouted for joy?" (Job 38:4, 7). God's performance at Creation was a showstopper that garnered a standing ovation.

Taking Time to Wonder

Before we'd moved away from Colorado, our family had sometimes placed sleeping bags on the deck of our home so we could spend the night out under the awe-inspiring summer sky. Listening to the oohs and aahs of my children sparked a sense of wonder in my own heart.

I realized how subtly but thoroughly cynicism, technological advancement, and the dogma of evolutionary scientists influence our adult minds. When we try to reduce God to something we can comprehend or a philosophy we can understand, our souls become numb to His preeminence and transcendence. When we're caught up in the constant activity and responsibilities of adult life, we must learn to consciously open our "child's" eyes to see the miraculous that surrounds us.

One evening, I wrapped my fuzzy-haired, five-year-old daughter, Joy, in a soft blanket and held her on our deck as we peered into the star-studded sky. Just then, a shooting star burst across the sky from one end to the other.

"Mama, how can anyone see this and not believe in God?" my little girl asked. "He painted the sky to make us happy."

Owning a sense of wonder at God's transcendence, acknowledging that He is above and beyond anything we can imagine, will inevitably increase the magnitude of our faith. If we are to serve Him in this world, we must humble ourselves before Him. We must bow our wills and lives before His ways, acknowledging that "as the heavens are higher than the earth, so are [His] ways higher than [our] ways and [His] thoughts than [our]

When we try to reduce God to something we can comprehend or a philosophy we can understand, our souls become numb to His preeminence and transcendence.

thoughts" (Isaiah 55:9). As I mentioned early in the book, my habit of looking at the infinite God out under the stars with Joy became a renewing practice in our lives.

When we fight this truth, we may find ourselves behaving like toddlers, shaking our fists and throwing tantrums when God does not work the way we think He should. From our limited perspective, we fret and stew when we do not understand what is happening. How grateful I am that God is not threatened by tantrums. After all, He has lived through the fist shaking and heartrending prayers of so many generations of His children. And because He is a good Father, He does not give in to our demands. He knows that His will is far better for us than our own and that He truly is able to work all things together for good for those of us who are called according to His purpose (see Romans 8:28).

Becoming like a Little Child

Jesus once told His disciples that unless they became "like little children, [they would] never get into the Kingdom of Heaven" (Matthew 18:3, NLT). One of my goals is to become more childlike the older I get.

From time to time, I do live in the audacious mind-set where I imagine, *What might God do through my life, in the power of the Holy Spirit, if I were willing to dream big and believe in miracles? What might He accomplish through me if I would only throw off my cloak of worry and just enjoy the beauty, dance with the invisible music, and celebrate life?*

At such times, I realize that I may miss out on His best when I am engrossed in my own projects. Maybe there were times when He wanted to give me a vacation, but I was busy thinking I had to fulfill everyone's needs or expectations. Perhaps there were times I was like Martha, working to exhaustion, while He was waiting for me to spend the day with Him on a picnic at a mountain lake.

Over the years, I've learned some ways to rest in the transcendence of God—particularly when I have lost sight of His glory because I'm so focused on my circumstances.

Bow Your Heart toward Christ

In my better times, I am more like Peter, who saw Jesus walking on the water and asked Him if he should get out of the boat and walk toward Him. "Come!" Jesus said (Matthew 14:28-29). As long as Peter kept his eyes on Jesus, only the bottoms of his feet got wet. But once he saw the strong wind and the waves, he started to sink. He, at least, got out of the boat. Why, I wonder, am I so often determined to row my boat and get to shore under my own power rather than follow Christ's command to "walk on water" in some area of my life?

As the One who could tread across the water, turn a loaf of bread into dinner for five thousand, and keep the stars in place, He obviously wants us to think big, to worship worthily, and to bask in His enormity. We can own our view of a mighty, miracle-working God when we choose to take our eyes off ourselves and focus on Him. I've begun to do so by asking God to help me change my attitude in two critical areas:

1. I have learned to revise the "What ifs" I ask myself. When I fret over questions like, *What if we run out of money? What if one of the kids has a wreck on the snowy freeway? What if I become terminally ill? What if the planes are grounded and we miss our flight to the conference?* I am focusing on possible problems, not on our Problem Solver. Not only that, but most of my worries never come to pass.

   The what-if questions I want to ask reflect childlike wonder and provide rest for my soul. *What if God has blessing ahead of me? What if I wait on Him, knowing His ways are so much bigger than mine? What if He is preparing to open a Red Sea for me? What if He still wants to do miracles? What might God do through me if I speak a word in gentleness or serve someone generously?*

   I work as faithfully in my daily life as I know how, but I live as though I need God to show up. As I do, I have learned that God loves to be generous. He orchestrates all sorts of provisions, power, and blessing on my behalf whenever I look to Him with the innocent faith of a child.

2. I have learned the importance of living with an attitude of humility. God cannot play His proper role as my Creator, King, Lord, and Holy One if I do not humble myself and see Him as He really is: the eternal (no beginning or ending), all-loving, omnipotent (all-powerful), omnipresent (in all places at all times), omniscient (all-knowing), and immutable (unchanging) God.

Until I acknowledge that I am limited in myself, I cannot fully grasp God's infinite greatness or be willing to submit to His will and His ways. I want to live with the same perspective as many in Scripture who walked into the presence of God. Have you ever noticed how they fell to their knees, knocked over by His glory?

When Moses encountered God in the burning bush, he "hid his face, for he was afraid to look at God" (Exodus 3:6). Isaiah saw the Lord sitting on His heavenly throne and cried out, "It's all over! I am doomed, for I am a sinful man. I have filthy lips, and I live among a people with filthy lips. Yet I have seen the King, the LORD of Heaven's Armies" (Isaiah 6:5, NLT). When standing on the mountain with the transfigured Jesus, Peter fell facedown on the ground in terror after hearing a booming voice proclaim, "This is My beloved Son, with whom I am well-pleased; listen to Him!" (Matthew 17:5-6).

God is so much bigger, more spectacular, and more glorious than any person can conceive. No wonder the first reaction of all these pious men was to be afraid, to fall down. For us to live beyond our present circumstances and into the grace of His provision and promises, we must recognize God as He truly is.

Even as the tiny, temporary lights of city streets, cars, and signs seem to snuff out the powerful stars, so the false lights and values of this world can darken our minds to the grandeur and brilliance of God. It's only when we see with the eyes of humble faith and bow before Him that we can hear His instructions: "He leads the humble in what is right, and teaches the humble his way" (Psalm 25:9, ESV). The apostle Peter also reminds us that it pays to be humble and to "clothe [ourselves] with humility toward one another, for 'God opposes the proud but gives grace to the humble'" (1 Peter 5:5, ESV).

Even as the tiny, temporary lights of city streets, cars, and signs seem to snuff out the powerful stars, so the false lights and values of this world can darken our minds to the grandeur and brilliance of God.

By giving His life, Jesus, of course, is the ultimate example of living humbly before our heavenly Father. The apostle Paul tells us we develop humility when we look to Him:

> Have this mind among yourselves, which is yours
> in Christ Jesus, who, though he was in the form of
> God, did not count equality with God a thing to be
> grasped, but emptied himself, by taking the form
> of a servant, being born in the likeness of men. And
> being found in human form, he humbled himself
> by becoming obedient to the point of death, even
> death on a cross. PHILIPPIANS 2:5-8, ESV

Own your heart's humility before God so that you can see Him in His proper place, bow your knee before His preeminence, and serve His purposes in your life: "Fear of the LORD teaches wisdom; humility precedes honor" (Proverbs 15:33, NLT). God will not share the throne of your heart, because He is the only one who rightfully belongs there.

Practice Worshiping Regularly

Cultivating a few daily rituals enables me to regularly reflect on God's greatness and gives me anchors of stability on even the busiest days. Almost every morning when I awaken, I brew a cup of tea or coffee and light a candle. It is my way of reminding myself and those around me that I am taking a few minutes of quiet time to start my day.

Next I turn on music, whether on my phone, my iPad, or my computer. Over the years I have collected acoustic instrumental albums, and their music sets the mood to soothe my soul.

No matter where I am, whether traveling or at home, I sit in front of a window. Nature always draws me away from my universe of self to the bigger picture in which God rules over all things. Whether I look out over a snowy field, a cloudy sky, the spring flowers, or a sunrise, I look for ways to acknowledge God's fingerprints in what I see. I am then better able to quiet my heart and turn my mind toward God.

I also read a part of a psalm each morning, circling each mention of one of God's attributes as I come across it. Often, I read from a daily Scripture book like *Daily Light on the Daily Path* that has verses for morning and night. Even on those days when I have only a few minutes for worship, these verses point my mind to truths about God. Several times a week, I take more time to read a longer passage from the New Testament, and I read through one complete book before starting another. My goal is not to check another book off my reading list but to look for passages that help me know God better, teach me how to obey Him, or illustrate the central point of one of Jesus' parables or stories. I then write down something I learned to take with me into my day.

I spend these minutes with God even if it means I have to get up early. I've made a personal rule not to allow myself to look at my e-mail, Facebook page, or blog until I have met with God. I also do not answer my phone, unless one of my children is calling. (I know they will never phone me early unless it is something important.) If I do not intentionally protect my early-morning, personal time with

God, inevitably I will be sidetracked by a phone call, the dog barking to get out the door, or an urgent deadline on my calendar.

As a young mom, I was so desperate to have time alone that I would go to sleep when my young children went to sleep and get up at an unreasonably early hour just to have this rest and peace. I did this even when it seemed that no matter how early I got up, my children sensed that I was awake and would get up too! At such times, I would put them in front of a Winnie the Pooh video or give them some new sidewalk chalk or a jar of bubbles. Instead of using that time to clean, I would sit down with my cup of tea to spend some time with the Lord. Cleaning is a never-ending task—so it was still there when I finished my ten minutes—but whatever it took, I made a little time every day for my soul.

These quiet moments of worship have always been a time to place my day and my circumstances into God's hands. When I begin this time by praising Him for one of His attributes, whether His love, sovereignty, kindness, or omnipresence, I am reminded that He is preeminent over all my circumstances. This puts God in His proper place and me in mine—His child dependent on Him.

Choose Thankfulness

I made a goal earlier in life to overcome difficulty by cultivating a heart attitude that recognizes that this place I am in is a place where I can worship God because He sees me and will show me His grace. One way that I developed this outlook was by envisioning myself lighting candles in dark places. That gave me a visual picture of who I wanted to become while living in a world separated from God's original design. I knew that this world is a broken place but that God has called His children to become redeemers—to reflect His wholeness, beauty, and goodness to others.

It was in that spirit that I recently wrote a short blog post about a delightful moment I shared with my older daughter, Sarah, when we were both at home on a wintry day. As gigantic snowflakes drifted softly into piles outside our window, we set a table with candles, scones, jam, and sour cream. I took a picture of our little table before we sat down together to drink tea from china cups in front of a roaring fire. Later I posted that picture alongside a blog post in which I'd written how happy I was to have celebrated a few moments with my daughter amidst all the deadlines and busyness of my life just then.

I received a scathing response from a young woman who accused me of not understanding the realities of most women. After noting that she spent each day with several whiny children in a messy house while wondering how she would ever pay all her bills, she wrote, "You may think you are encouraging women out there, but you just make me feel inadequate, and I am never going to read your blog again. And you can take this comment off the blog if you don't want to let the truth be known to others who feel like me!"

My first impulse was to write to let her know how I've had to endure seventeen moves, health issues with my children, devastating church splits, a fire in our home, inadequate health insurance, criticism from family, and the long hours, travel, and financial strains that come with launching a ministry. I surprised even myself at the speed with which I could name the many difficulties and challenges our family has lived through.

Fortunately, a few seconds later, God prompted me to pray for this woman instead. As I did, my sanity returned, and I was again grateful to have had that rare one-on-one time with my daughter in the middle of an otherwise demanding day. My habit of choosing to be thankful and learning to be content and loving had served as an "accountability partner" to draw me back to what was true.

I am convinced that gratefulness is a life changer. It does not come naturally to us, because as fallen creatures we always want more, more, more. And yet practicing thankfulness will change our attitudes. It also transforms the patterns our brains follow. When we frequently think the same thoughts, we are actually making roadways, paths, and ruts in our brains.

Those well-worn thought paths determine the first place our brains go in a new situation. If you spend too much time being ungrateful for what you have, you will become whiny and complaining. Inevitably, such an attitude will diminish your faith and darken your attitude toward life. Before long, it will become an actual "habit" of your mind. The same is true for thankfulness. If you choose to accept whatever comes with a trusting and grateful heart, you will exude peace and joy. The more you practice thoughts and attitudes of gratitude, the stronger will be the habit of thankfulness in your mind. Whatever you water will grow.

One way I've trained my heart and mind to develop a habit of gratitude is by filling journals with everything I can be thankful for, including the many ways I've observed God's faithfulness. I remember that I am not a victim of my circumstances and that the God who has not abandoned me before will not abandon me now in any present difficulties.

Cultivate Your Inner Child Heart and Celebrate Life!

Our world disdains virtue and purity, prefers doubt and rationality to faith, and is suspicious of anyone who trusts in a God who rules above all, is daily involved in the affairs of men, and is coming back to take us to a spectacular new heaven and earth.

Yet it was Jesus who said, "My Kingdom is not of this world" (John 18:36, NLT). Rarely do I meet women who are unburdened, who choose to live in freedom, grace, and beauty. But when I do, I feel that I have been in the presence of Jesus. Their exuberance in this dark world reminds me of one of my favorite quotes, which is attributed to Friedrich Nietzsche: "Those who were seen dancing were thought to be insane by those who could not hear the music."

I love this quote because I want to be one of those people who dances to God's invisible music—that invisible reality where God works in response to His children's prayers, where angels dance, and where heaven prepares a glorious banquet for those just naive enough to believe in a Hero who will take us to a heaven where the celebration will never end.

Our God delights to find even one such person. Own your sense of wonder, and the celebration of the stars and the unseen blessings of your life will always bring you a secret delight, an unquenchable song, and a bubbling joy that this world will never be able to quench.

✻

Own Your Part

I was awash with weariness. Tension was giving me a neck ache, as I was anxious about meeting several deadlines as well as three weeks of impending company. One morning I rose early and drove thirty minutes to a five-star hotel near my home that is built next to a little lake.

I ordered a cappuccino, found a shady spot in front of the lake, and sipped in the coffee and the peace and beauty of a Colorado mountain morning. I sauntered slowly around the lake a couple of times. Finally, as I was driving home, I put on an album of some of my favorite music, and after my two hours of getting away from it all, got lost in the melodies.

When I got home, all the deadlines were still there, but my spirit was much changed. My little mini-rest had changed me so that I was better able to face the next few weeks.

1. What is the biggest emotional drainer in your life? How can you place it in God's hands and step back to get a better picture of how you might deal with it?

2. Read this verse: "Let the peace of Christ rule in your hearts, to which indeed you were called in one body; and be thankful" (Colossians 3:15).

What is ruling your thoughts instead of the peace of Christ? You were called to live in peace. What false light is hiding your issues from the light of God's power and commitment to lighten your load and walk you through your circumstances with His strength and wisdom?

3. Plan a time when you can get away from the concrete, noise, and demands of your world. Look for a place in creation where you can rest your whole self. It might be a hike in the mountains, a day at the beach, or a picnic in the park. Be sure to get away often enough that you are regularly exposed to God's art and able to remember that He is transcendent above all the details of your life.

Praying with You

Lord of the mountains and the sea, take these precious ones away from the daily pressures and demands of life to a place of quiet where they might see Your eternal and transcendent beauty and rest there for some time. Take their burdens and give them peace. We love You. Amen.

CHAPTER 7

ALLOWING GOD'S SPIRIT TO BREATHE IN YOU

Owning the Holy Spirit's Strength through Your Life

Spiritual transformation is primarily the work of the Holy Spirit. He is the Master Sculptor.   JERRY BRIDGES

[Jesus] breathed on them and said, "Receive the Holy Spirit."
JOHN 20:22, NLT

I SAT IN A SMALL SAILBOAT ON A VAST LAKE, marveling at the thousands of diamond lights that seemed to bob up and down on the surface of the turquoise water, sparkling with a thousand rainbow colors. We swayed gently back and forth to the rhythm of small waves thrumming against our craft. Closing my eyes, I felt drowsiness creep slowly over me as the gentle movement nearly rocked me to sleep.

As the chilly morning breezes picked up and blew across the water, I was grateful to be shackled within the tethers of my life jacket. "This wind is a gift on such a beautiful day," my friend said as he began to hoist the heavy silk sails up the tall mast.

I opened my eyes just in time to see him wield the helm. Suddenly, as the wind filled our sails, our boat shot forward, sliding smoothly and swiftly over the water. I felt as though we were flying as we sliced through the bouncing waves. Feelings of exhilaration spontaneously bubbled up into laughter. Once our sails captured the wind, we were no longer sitting stuck and still in the water; instead, we were sailing effortlessly across the lake.

How we all long to sail through life with such ease and grace, flying through our days with the supernatural hand of God over all the details of our lives. Yet often we stay dead in the water, with no hope of moving forward as we depend on our own power to row forward. We may even diligently try pushing our oars against the tension of the waters that press about us, laboring to make progress in the Christian life through our own great efforts.

God created us to soar, to dance, to fly—to live with gusto as we enjoy and discover the magnificence of the mysteries He has strewn through creation. He longs for us to hear His whispers throughout the day, to see the shadows of His ways moment by moment. But not only that; He also promises to walk with us through each day. Just as the sails caught the wind, letting the boat glide effortlessly through the water, so when our hearts are filled with the Spirit of God, we move ahead through life unburdened and with more ease.

Have you ever felt a stirring in your heart as a touching story brought tears to your eyes or as you heard a soaring symphony or a captivating song on the radio that opened a new window in your soul? Maybe you have felt a similar exhilaration while watching a sunset, camping out under the night sky, or holding a newborn babe. Something inside of you quickened, and for a moment, some heavenly beauty connected your inner self with the divine. C. S. Lewis referred to such experiences as joy. These are remnants and reminders of the perfect world God designed for us to live in—the shadow of places He longs to take us to, the reality of the other world He's preparing for us.

When Jesus gave His life to pay the debt for our sins, He did not do it just so we could go to heaven. He wanted us to experience newness of life now, to feel the relief that comes from a fresh start. That's what He meant when He said, "I came that they may have life, and have it abundantly" (John 10:10).

Even the Old Testament speaks of God's desire to be a resource of great blessing in our lives. David, a man after God's own heart, said, "Taste and see that the LORD is good; how blessed is the man who takes refuge in Him!" (Psalm 34:8).

Too many believers experience the Christian life as a work to be done, a duty to perform, a list of things to be checked off. Yet our works always fall short. Whenever we consider how well we have given, served, loved, or shared the gospel, we feel disappointed because we think God is disappointed with us. Does this really reflect the heart of God?

Every year, I rise early on the morning of each of my children's birthdays to bake homemade cinnamon rolls and prepare a favorite egg-and-cheese dish. I set these out on our table, along with fresh fruit. I shop early so I have time to carefully choose presents that will suit their individual tastes. I do this for every one of my children because I delight in each of them and want to tangibly express my love. I never say, "You cannot have a birthday breakfast this year if you have had a bad attitude, or if you have not washed enough dishes, or if you have cost me too much money." I want to lavish my love on them as a way to validate their worth, give them pleasure, and show them my love, which is not dependent on their behavior.

God is much more loving and generous than I am. He lavishes His love on us in many tangible ways. We see it in the beauty of nature and the sense of purpose inside each one of us. We do not deserve His generosity, and we are beyond blessed to have such a heavenly Father.

Works Do Not Prove Our Spirituality

Our works do not earn us God's presence or favor. Depending on them is a losing battle because we will never, in our own flesh, be able to live up to the law's standard. The best we can do is to gut it out in the midst of our innate selfishness and immaturity as we try living by rules and works in a hopeless effort to be "good enough."

Thankfully, God never called us to live a "good Christian life" based on effort and rule keeping. He wants us to experience His magnificent personality, not just know the rules He handed down. We are fully alive only when we seek to hear the melody of His song and see the treasures that yield a clue to His majesty. To live only within the mundane constrictions of daily life is not to be alive at all.

Christian means "Christ in one." When we live in Him, we are "in Christ Jesus." When I learned this secret—owning the Holy Spirit's strength in my life—I was transformed. Christians cannot flourish apart from making God's Spirit the source of their spiritual lives. Even the phrase "spiritual life" refers to the Spirit-living-through-us life.

To live only within the mundane constrictions of daily life is not to be alive at all.

I am not speaking of some kind of unique charismatic experience (though throughout history, people have experienced God's filling in different ways), but of a power that we can never muster up on our own. It might be described as:

an inner strength
a voice that calls us to become more excellent
an energy that moves us to love and forgive supernaturally
a fruitfulness that can only be explained by God

When the Holy Spirit directs our course, the natural consequence is a life outside of normal striving or fleshly effort. We are able to live beyond our own capacity.

Throughout Scripture, Jesus compares the Holy Spirit to the blowing wind. When talking with Nicodemus, the Pharisee, Jesus said that when one is born again, it happens by the Spirit. "The wind blows where it wishes and you hear the sound of it, but do not know where it comes from and where it is going; so is everyone who is born of the Spirit" (John 3:8). We can't touch or contain the Spirit, but we can see evidence of Him in the lives of His followers.

On rare occasions, I have met people with the palpable fragrance of Christ's Spirit about them. I was thirteen weeks pregnant and began to hemorrhage not long after my husband, three young children, and I had moved to Nashville. I had not yet had time to find a physician, and as my husband and I were trying to decide what to do, a neighbor I did not know well offered to call a midwife to help take care of me.

Heather, the angel who arrived at my door, was a total stranger who cared for me as I went through that traumatic miscarriage, and she waited with me after an ambulance had been called to take me to the hospital. The mercy and tenderness with which she cared for my ravaged body were almost supernatural. She washed me as I lay nearly unconscious in my bathtub, using such gentle words and such a kind touch that her love enveloped me. I have never forgotten the comfort of being in her presence.

As a young missionary, I worked with a man who was about twenty years my senior. Whenever we were together, I felt a burning desire inside to live better, to trust more, and to give my life more generously to Kingdom work. This man exhibited the life of Christ, and his contagious excitement for living was almost palpable.

I have another friend whom I seek out because I know that when I am with her, I will want to be my best self. Throughout her years of daily devotions, she has invested so much time studying Scripture that each word she speaks comes from a depth of wisdom. When Christ lives in us, there will be a similar manifestation of His supernatural life pulsing through us.

All three of these people's unique personalities were expressed, even as they made God's love more real to me. Whenever Jesus lives through someone, the attributes of God's personality are clearly expressed and experienced.

My personal experiences are reminiscent of the time when Jesus, who had just been resurrected from the dead, began walking and talking with some men who were on their way to Emmaus. After discussing Scriptures, they sat down to eat, and Jesus broke bread and gave it to them. Only at that moment did they realize who He was, and then He vanished from their sight. They said to one another, "Were not our hearts burning within us while He was speaking to us on the road, while He was explaining the Scriptures to us?" (Luke 24:32). Christ's presence awakened in them an excitement about God's fulfillment of Scripture through Jesus. Their hearts thrilled in His companionship.

In an earlier chapter, I mentioned the resurrected Jesus' appearance to the disciples on Easter eve (John 20:19-22). "Peace be with you," He told them. As He prepared them to go out and proclaim the gospel, He promised peace in the midst of their work, peace in the midst of their storms, peace—always! Then He breathed His breath of life on them and told this group of intimate friends, "Receive the Holy Spirit."

Jesus recognized that even the disciples, His most committed followers, were spiritually dead and helpless. Without the Holy Spirit, they would never be sensitive to His wisdom. And so He had to breathe into them the very breath of His life. He does the same inside each of us when we become Christians. We are not alone, dependent on our own resources to live our lives, to do His work. When we walk in the Spirit, we are moved to think what Jesus would think and to do what Jesus would do. Only the Holy Spirit can develop the motivations and character of Christ inside us, little by little making us into the new creations that we were originally designed to be.

When we walk in the Spirit, we are moved to think what Jesus would think and to do what Jesus would do.

Too often I hear from women who are striving in their own strength, carrying burdens of guilt from past failures and fearful of life and the stresses of what might happen, trying to find the right formula to create happiness. But the reality is, none of us can live life well without Jesus at the center, restoring what we have lost. But what is the secret to walking in the Spirit? I have pondered this ten-million-dollar question for years.

How to Walk in the Spirit

Scripture tells us that Jesus grew in wisdom and stature and in favor with God and man (see Luke 2:52). He went through the natural human process of developing from a tiny baby into a grown man. We also acquire spiritual maturity and strength by walking with the Spirit over many years. We start out in our faith as baby Christians, and the more we learn to yield our thoughts, our sins, our fears, our dreams into the hands of God, the more we grow and bear the fruit of the Holy Spirit.

Scripture uses walking as a metaphor for pursuing the path of life. Paul, for instance, said, "Walk by the Spirit, and you will not carry out the desire of the flesh" (Galatians 5:16).

Walking by the Spirit means yielding our thoughts, attitudes, desires, prayers, and goals to the Spirit as we go about our days. For me, this works itself out in the prayers I so often shoot up to God:

"God, I give this day to You. Will You guide my thoughts, prompt me in Your wisdom, and lead me to behave in a way that pleases You? And let me know when I am getting off track."

"Lord, I am so angry and frustrated with this person. I know You want me to change my attitude and choose to love her. Will You calm my anger and give me the will to show her Your love?"

"Lord, we do not know how we are going to pay our bills this month, but I do not have the capacity to change our situation or the energy to worry about this. Will You please take care of this burden? Will You please provide us with enough money or another job?"

"God, it is snowing tonight, and my new teenage driver is driving on the freeway out in the storm. You have access to her brain. Will You please remind her to slow down, and will You protect her while she drives?"

After voicing such a prayer, I mentally give my burden to God and let Him take it. If I start to worry again, I acknowledge that He is in control. I then praise Him for His compassion and ability to take care of the situation. And I choose not to worry. It is a choice of my will to obey Him, trust Him, talk to Him, and leave my burden in His hands each moment.

Just as I hand the Holy Spirit my burdens and concerns, so must I yield my attitudes, desires, and actions to Him. Shortly before His crucifixion, Jesus discussed with His disciples how we do this: "Abide in Me, and I in you. As the branch cannot bear fruit of itself unless it abides in the vine, so neither can you unless you abide in Me" (John 15:4).

It's all about your heart. Are you yielding yourself to Christ each moment because you love Him and desire to please Him? When that is truly the desire of your heart, you will begin to exhibit His life in your circumstances. As the apostle Paul reminds us, "Those who are dominated by the sinful nature think about sinful things, but those who are controlled by the Holy Spirit think about things that please the Spirit" (Romans 8:5, NLT).

Discipline your thoughts so that when they are moving in the direction of sin, you can dwell on the things that please God instead. Remember the truth you have learned in God's Word: "If you are living according to the flesh, you must die; but if by the Spirit you are putting to death the deeds of the body, you will live" (Romans 8:13).

Living in the Spirit is an active choice of your will. He will not force Himself on you. Even as you choose to stop at a red light because you know it is the right thing to do, you can stop giving in to your flesh—your striving, jealousy, pettiness—with the help of God's Spirit. Whenever He convicts you of sin, consider it a red light and turn your heart to obey Him. He is within you to help you learn how to live in the freedom of His love and wisdom.

Galatians 5:22-23 defines the fruit of the Spirit as "love, joy, peace, patience, kindness, goodness, faithfulness, gentleness, self-control."

Rather than thinking of each attribute as a different kind of fruit—an apple, an orange, a pear, etc.—I remember that a single piece of fruit, like an apple, can have different attributes. Though it could accurately be described as crispy, sweet, smooth, red, round, and firm, it is still one piece of fruit. Similarly, the word *fruit*, in this verse, refers to one fruit with many attributes. As you and I grow in Christ and dwell in fellowship and agreement with the Spirit of Jesus inside us, all of these attributes grow bigger and stronger, even as an apple grows from a blossom into a fully ripe apple that is ready to be picked. As God's Spirit works in our lives, we will be progressively more reflective of all He is.

Living by guilt is a waste of His precious sacrifice and provision. When we celebrate His desire to bless us and provide for us because we are His beloved children, it pleases Him. His Spirit accepts each of us as we are and leads us to maturity as we listen to Him and obey Him. His Spirit assures us of His love when we feel guilty, helping us live in the freedom of grace.

We are all works in process. Rather than trying to be perfect in our own strength, God calls us to rest in Him. To learn from Him. To practice loving through Him. To talk to Him. We can strive to become more like one of the first followers of God, a man named Enoch. Genesis 5:22-24 introduces us to this godly man who walked closely with God for nearly four hundred years—living in companionship with Him along life's way, receiving His love and listening to His wisdom.

Though I don't expect to live half as long as Enoch did, I do hope that the older I get, the more it can be said of me, "Sally walks with God. You can see Him in the way she lives, the words she speaks, the peace and humility she has about her, and the way she depends on Him. When you are with her, you feel like you have been with Him."

When Jesus becomes your focus, your love, your defining voice, your generosity, your grace, and when you allow His Spirit to live freely in you, then, and only then, will you have the energy and wisdom to live the Christian life well. It is His work, and He will kindly carry your load.

✳

Own Your Part

As I was working in my home office recently, my laptop shut off and would not come back on. After verifying that the cord was plugged into the power strip, I asked Joel, my resident Apple expert, to help me try to fix it.

We both became frustrated when, no matter what we attempted to do, my computer would not restart. Unbeknownst to us, someone had accidentally unplugged the power strip from the wall, so my computer was separated from its source of power. Even though my computer has the potential to connect to the world through the Internet, to receive e-mail messages, to serve me as I write and store books there, it is still totally useless to me when it's disconnected from its power source. Likewise, no matter our potential for living fully, when we are disconnected from our power source, the Holy Spirit, it is impossible to live fully and to live well.

1. God's Word is the language He uses to speak to me. The passages I have memorized over the years constantly speak to me in the moments of my day. To tap into the power of Scripture, choose five verses of Scripture that encourage you and memorize them this month. Start with this verse: "Walk by the Spirit, and you will not carry out the desire of the flesh" (Galatians 5:16).

2. Practicing good habits enables us to respond well to challenging life situations. Every day before you get out of bed, make it a habit to pray to God and acknowledge that He is with you

and loves you. Speak to Him throughout your day, inviting His Spirit to live through you. The more you talk to Him, the more you will be filled with His words, wisdom, and strength.

3. Romans 8:1-2 says, "There is now no condemnation for those who are in Christ Jesus. For the law of the Spirit of life in Christ Jesus has set you free from the law of sin and of death."

    Each of us daily falls short of the righteous ways in which we would like to live. Begin practicing living in light of the truth of Romans 8:1-2. Because you are in Christ, you are not condemned by God. The Spirit of Life, the Holy Spirit, has set you free from the bondage of death. Breathe in that truth today— there is no condemnation for you because of His Spirit in your life today. Live in His grace.

Praying with You

Dear Precious Lord, we need You every moment of our lives. Help us to struggle with the pressures of life less and allow Your Spirit to blow through our attitudes, our hearts, and what we value, and teach us how to leave our burdens in Your hands. We bow our wills to Yours because You are the only One who can live the Christian life through us. Amen.

PART 4

Owning Your Life by Partnering with God

Attitudes and Actions That Transform

CHAPTER 8

CULTIVATING THE PRACTICES THAT DEEPEN YOUR FAITH

Owning the Spiritual Disciplines

In prayer it is better to have a heart without words, than words without a heart.
ATTRIBUTED TO JOHN BUNYAN

[Jesus] said to them, "The Scriptures declare, 'My Temple will be called a house of prayer.'" MATTHEW 21:13, NLT

HOLDING BABY JOY CLOSE TO MY CHEST, I sat taut against the uncomfortable bathtub faucet. Joel and Nathan were also squished onto my lap, and Clay sat right next to me, with Sarah perched on top of his folded legs.

Minutes before, a deputy from the local sheriff's office had called to let us know that a tornado was racing directly toward our home in the country. Even before his call, the winds had begun howling and the sky had turned purple and black.

From outside the relative safety of the tub, we heard the sounds of shutters banging wildly and flying debris pinging against the windows. The deep groan of the wind drowned the shouts of our voices as Clay and I tried to soothe the mounting fear we saw in our children's faces.

At ages twelve, nine, seven, and six months, they stared wide-eyed at Clay and me. They seemed to be looking for any signs of panic on our faces, as though we were a barometer of how fearful they should be. Suddenly Joel, our skinny, slight, older son, stood to the full height of his three-foot-ten-inch frame and shouted earnestly, "Have I not commanded you? Be strong and courageous! Do not tremble or be dismayed, for the Lord your God is with you wherever you go!" The others, having it in their minds also, began shouting the words of Joshua 1:9 with him, over and over again. Their chant became a game that led to smiles on their faces as they confidently yelled it into the suffocating noise of the winds. It was the Word of God alive in a little boy's heart, pushing out into the reality of the terrifying moment until the storm had passed.

Just the month before, my normally fear-prone son had come upon a large, black, furry spider in his attic bedroom. He screamed and ran down the stairs to get us. After Clay had rid the room of the "monster," I sat on the bunk beds with my little boys, who were lying together, and told them that throughout their lives, they would encounter fears, challenges, and scary moments.

"What I want you to remember is that you are never alone!" I told them. "God will always be with you. He wants you to see His fingerprints and hear His voice in your hearts wherever you go because you are so very precious to Him. He is watching over you because you are His sons."

I told them the story of Joshua, Moses' assistant and his successor as the Israelites' leader, who had to lead about two million men, women, and children into a land of giants. Joshua and his men would have to defeat these enemies before they could build their homes and settle there.

"How would you feel going into battle against such strong armies?" I asked.

"Real, real scared!" Joel answered with childish sincerity.

"Sweet boy, God has made you and Nathan with hearts that can be bold and courageous for Him. I am going to teach you a new Bible verse—a promise that God gave to Joshua—and I want you to say it out loud and always remember that God will give you strength to face any moment of fear that comes your way!"

And so, repeatedly, the two boys and I spoke Joshua 1:9 aloud until I knew it was secure in their memory: "Have I not commanded you? Be strong and courageous! Do not tremble or be dismayed, for the Lord your God is with you wherever you go."

And in the next moment of crisis, God's Word spoke to my young son, and he became a pillar of strength for us all. I have often seen the Word of God speak to my exact situation: in times of relational struggle, times of fear, times when I needed wisdom, times of darkness, times of great joy. Scripture provides an apt word for any situation in my life.

God doesn't want us to guess at the purposes of life or how we should live. He wants us to know His presence in our beginnings, endings, and all in between. He never intended us to feel scared, helpless, hopeless, or clueless. The Lord wants to be a companion to us through every part of life, and the spiritual disciplines are a means of spending time with Him so we can know Him better.

Understanding the Value of Spiritual Disciplines

My younger daughter now goes to college, a couple thousand miles away from home. Providentially named Joy, she makes me giggle as she tells stories of her adventures with gusto. She also enjoys sharing all the deep ideas she is thinking about and the insights she is learning about God. Recently when she called, she said, "Mama, I think I am becoming you. My thoughts sound a lot like your voice, and the advice I give to others includes the same messages I have heard my whole life. Here at school I am known for drinking strong black tea, reading lots of books, and lighting candles, as though that is something unusual. I guess all those years of living with you have worn off on me!"

Because God is relational, He desires that we understand and know

Him—the same desires I have for my relationship with Joy. Even as we would not feel close to someone with whom we rarely invested time or conversation, so we cannot feel close to God if we do not regularly commune with Him, getting to know Him and His ways and listening attentively to His voice. When we spend lots of time with Him, He rubs off on us and we start looking a lot more like Him.

All of the traditional spiritual disciplines (such as studying God's Word, praying, and celebrating Sabbath rest) are designed to help us recognize and honor the preciousness of our relationship with God. These practices make us aware of His presence. We must make an investment of time and effort if we want to experience His blessing, favor, wisdom, comfort, and pleasure. We cannot develop a spiritually strong life apart from Him.

God sent the Old Testament prophet Jeremiah to entreat His people in Judah to return to Him. He reminded His wayward people where their true strength came from:

> Thus says the LORD, "Let not a wise man boast of his
> wisdom, and let not the mighty man boast of his might, let
> not a rich man boast of his riches; but let him who boasts
> boast of this, *that he understands and knows Me*, that I am the
> LORD who exercises lovingkindness, justice and righteousness
> on earth; for I delight in these things," declares the LORD.
> JEREMIAH 9:23-24, ITALICS ADDED

Like the Judeans, we are prone to rely on our own wisdom, power, or intelligence to navigate life. That leaves us extremely vulnerable. We cannot have the wisdom to own our life choices and behave prudently if we do not have God's Word informing our thoughts. It is impossible to be godly and mature without spending extensive time with God.

In his book *Life with God*, Richard Foster explains that the spiritual disciplines put us "in a position to receive from God the power to do what we cannot accomplish on our own."[3] That is why investing time in studying and familiarizing yourself with the voice and wisdom of God is foundational to owning your life. Taking responsibility for this area is prerequisite to living an intentional life and witnessing the power of God. If you have time for television but not for personal time with the Father, then you don't understand the value of your relationship with Him. If you spend hours on the Internet each week but rarely open your Bible, you are not committed to the honor of knowing and listening to Him.

The Whys of Studying the Word of God

Most of us have heard the admonition many times: Have devotionals, study God's Word, pray. But it's so hard to be consistent.

I don't have the time.

Life gets in the way.

Maybe you've had these thoughts too. Both have been issues in my own life at times. Yet studying the Bible is not just one more duty to fulfill or another spiritual work to be done. In fact, God does not want us to meet with Him just so we can check something else off our list. He is not trying to make our lives busier. Instead, He longs to live in authentic relationship with us.

I am a friend-oriented person. Life is best lived when shared in moments with one of my inner-circle peeps. I like meeting one-on-one with a friend because it provides such a richer experience of camaraderie:

Looking into her eyes so I can see her expression and response to
    what I am saying
Having a hand to hold
Embracing as a way to say, "I am so thankful for you"
Giggling over words too silly to say out loud to others
Sharing tears of despair and being understood and not
    condemned
Reading a beautiful story together
Watching a romantic movie and wishing life were that way

Watching a sunset
Sharing a feast over stimulating conversation

The One who imagined this kind of friendship is the One who wants such a friendship with us. God is a lover and friend by nature. He is a Father who cares. He designed intimacy as a longing of our hearts because He values relationship and wants to fulfill that need by becoming intimate with us.

In naming His Son the Word, our heavenly Father emphasized His desire to talk to us.

In naming His Son the Word, our heavenly Father emphasized His desire to talk to us. Talking implies a two-way conversation. From the creation of man, God has desired to be the constant companion of the children He shaped in His image. As He walked in the Garden with Adam and Eve, He surely enjoyed talking with them and sharing the beauty He had so elegantly and lovingly arranged.

The same is true for us today. God wants to walk with us and be our companion throughout life. It is not about a work to be done, but about intimacy and sharing life with the One who loves us and cares for us most. When we spend time in the living presence of the divine, our lives will be transformed. Living with an awareness of the King of kings will impact our very being.

The most significant habit in my own life has been filling my mind and heart with the Word of God. It has fueled every good work I have ever accomplished.

Once my son observed, "Mom, I was thinking about your area of expertise. Assuming you have had 300 to 320 quiet times each year—because no one has a quiet time every single day of the year!—and you have been doing them for over forty years, that means you have already spent over ten thousand hours studying your Bible and praying. I know that, on top of that, you have spent many untold hours preparing to teach. That makes you an expert in Scripture, according to this book I'm reading about what it takes to become a leader in any field."

His evaluation made me want to keep going. A great estate is built one brick at a time, and so my legacy in Scripture is being built one quiet time at a time. Though I went to church as a child, no one ever taught me how to study the Bible, so it was daunting to me then because I did not know where to start. When I was in college, a young woman taught me how to understand the Bible and how to begin studying God's Word a little at a time. Everyone has to start somewhere!

Understanding the Value of the Bible

While I can speak of the wisdom and strength I've gained personally from reading the Bible regularly, you don't have to take my word for it. It's fascinating to consider what the Bible itself says about the benefits of reading Scripture:

- God's Word will make you prosper and succeed.

  This book of the law shall not depart from your mouth,
  but you shall meditate on it day and night, so that you may
  be careful to do according to all that is written in it; for
  then you will make your way prosperous, and then you will
  have success. JOSHUA 1:8

- God's Word will show you how to make decisions and plans along your journey.

  Your word is a lamp to my feet and a light to my path.
  PSALM 119:105

- God's Word is as essential as food is in sustaining your life.

  [Jesus] answered and said, "It is written, 'Man shall not live
  on bread alone, but on every word that proceeds out of the
  mouth of God.'" MATTHEW 4:4

- God's Word is the true source for helping you persevere in challenging times and for giving you hope.

  Whatever was written in earlier times was written for our instruction, so that through perseverance and the encouragement of the Scriptures we might have hope. ROMANS 15:4

- God's Word is alive to counsel us, make us sharp, and help us evaluate issues of the heart in our own lives and in our dealings with others.

  The word of God is living and active and sharper than any two-edged sword, and piercing as far as the division of soul and spirit, of both joints and marrow, and able to judge the thoughts and intentions of the heart.   HEBREWS 4:12

- To be effective Christian leaders, we must accurately understand and apply God's Word.

  Be diligent to present yourself approved to God as a workman who does not need to be ashamed, accurately handling the word of truth.   2 TIMOTHY 2:15

  All Scripture is inspired by God and profitable for teaching, for reproof, for correction, for training in righteousness.   2 TIMOTHY 3:16

The Bible is God's voice in our lives. God's Word is His vocabulary, which He uses to speak to us daily along life's paths. If we have little Scripture stored in the recesses of our hearts and minds, we will have little wisdom to advise us in those moments when we need God's help.

Prayer

Meditative prayer is growing in popularity, particularly since studies have shown that meditation, worship, and thankfulness lower blood pressure, strengthen us physically, and restore peace and emotional stability.[4] God knows what He is doing when He invites us to talk with Him.

Yet struggling to know just what it means to pray to God is an age-old issue. Even Jesus' disciples asked how to pray (see Luke 11:1). He then gave them a simple pattern to follow.

Pray then like this:

Our Father in heaven,
hallowed be your name.
Your kingdom come,
your will be done,
  on earth as it is in heaven.
Give us this day our daily bread,
and forgive us our debts,
  as we also have forgiven our debtors.
And lead us not into temptation,
  but deliver us from evil.

MATTHEW 6:9-13, ESV

Jesus invites His followers to address God as their Father, a personal name that reminds us of His loving relationship with us. We are to remember that He is holy and that even now He is orchestrating all world events. He also invites us to bring all our daily needs to Him, including our need for forgiveness (as well as our need to forgive others). Finally, we can turn to Him for help in overcoming the devil, as well as our own proclivity to sin.

Jesus kept the Lord's Prayer short and simple because He wanted prayer to come from the heart, the kind of conversation between devoted companions. Prayer is not just saying words; rather, God gives us prayer as a way to engage with Him in our hearts and minds amidst the stresses and pressures of our days.

Over five hundred verses in the Bible are given to prayer, which illustrates how much God values conversation with us. But not only that; He also wants us to expect Him to respond when we ask Him to fight our battles and carry our burdens.

Jesus once told a parable about a widow who kept appealing to an unscrupulous judge for help. The judge was so tired of the woman's repeated pleas that he finally did what she asked. Jesus compared the uncaring judge with our heavenly Father. Since even a corrupt judge can be persuaded to rule for a helpless widow, Jesus says, "Will not God bring about justice for His elect who cry to Him day and night, and will He delay long over them? I tell you that He will bring about justice for them quickly. However, when the Son of Man comes, will He find faith on the earth?" (Luke 18:7-8). God does hear, and He does answer. Jesus' question—"will He find faith on the earth" when He returns—should encourage us to keep praying.

Sometimes I write "Dear Jesus" in a prayer journal and then pour out my heart to Him—my thanksgiving, requests, feelings, thoughts—all of me. Other days, I go through the list of my children's needs. Often, as my children were growing up, we would pray together every morning and every night.

Spontaneous prayer is a tradition in our family as well. "Thank You so much, Lord, for painting us such a beautiful sunset tonight." Or "Lord, please give the doctors and emergency staff wisdom to help that man in the wreck we just saw. Comfort all who are involved." And then other times, we pray with friends who are gathered in our home for Bible studies or holidays.

Daily I think of His words. I don't always feel like praying, and I sometimes wonder if I am just talking to the walls. Yet I've learned that God is not on my time schedule. Sometimes it has taken many years for me to see His answers to my prayers. Honestly, I often wish He would just hurry up! Not only that, His ways are also often different from mine, and He does not always do things my way. But I know with patience I will see the beautiful purpose in His workings.

I pray in humility to the transcendent God, who is above and beyond all my seemingly insurmountable circumstances, leaving the results in His hands. I worship Him, knowing that He is trustworthy. Just as toddlers don't always "feel" like obeying their parents, we will not always feel like praying. We do it because we trust God to be a loving Father who provides for His children. In the discipline of seeking God and observing His fingerprints in our lives, our hearts grow deeper, our souls better understand eternity, and we grow in awe of His personal care and love for us.

Choosing Rest to Stay Spiritually Alive

Telling someone we are weary is almost a badge of honor in this society, a culture that values "doing" far more than "being." Meeting deadlines, running ourselves (or our kids) to activities, checking off chores, cooking meals—all this busyness regularly drains us. And then there are the crises: illness, moving, out-of-town company, and all sorts of emergencies that unexpectedly demand all our focus and energy.

When we're young, we often believe we have no limits, and we never evaluate the consequences of living in an exhausted state all the time. As I look back on my sixty years, I can honestly say that I have never completed all my tasks, met all my deadlines, or finished my to-do lists—never, not even during one year. But no matter our age, women who live with no margins will eventually come to emotional, mental, and physical harm.

I realize that rest may seem like the least productive thing we can do when life is busy. It may not seem like a spiritual discipline, but more like an optional priority. Unless we believe in the goodness of God's character, we will find it difficult to place all that we are carrying and worrying about—including our to-do lists—into His hands. Yet only then will we begin to find peace. In fact, making time to rest may very well be our most strategic option when we have busy, full, and demanding lives. Without it, we will never grow in spiritual depth.

Although our culture seems to worship being busy, constant activity will slowly undermine our perspective on life and kill our souls. When we are preoccupied with our work, we almost always exclude the person right in our midst who is hoping for relationship. Sometimes when we are shouldering too much responsibility, we worry and start to fret. Sinking under the weight of so much to do with so little time zaps our energy. God always seems farther away, life's pressures feel unbearable, and our reactions to people, including our loved ones, become harsh when we live in a state of constant exhaustion. Eventually, we will likely end up with a serious illness, a bad attitude, and a frustrated faith.

Constant activity will slowly undermine our perspective on life and kill our souls.

When I see the telltale consequences of fatigue and burnout in myself, I try to find time to create margin in my life by evaluating areas where I can cut back and say no, giving myself time for refreshment and restoration. Life is a very long marathon, and if we are to finish well, we must consider how to pace ourselves along the way.

God first introduced His people to the Sabbath on their way to the Promised Land. When explaining why the people should gather twice as much manna on the sixth day as on the other days of the week, Moses said, "This is what the LORD commanded: Tomorrow will be a day of complete rest, a holy Sabbath day set apart for the LORD" (Exodus 16:23, NLT). Then God told Moses, "The Sabbath is the LORD's gift to you" (verse 29). God designed humans to stop at regular intervals, both to worship Him and to rest their bodies and minds. He put Sabbath rest into the weeks of our lives for a purpose.

But the Sabbath is not just a Sunday thing—it is a principle of stopping whenever life has drained us. To find the rest we need, we must build rhythms into life that include periods of quiet, times to stop each day.

When my children were little, I would do whatever I could to free just a few minutes for me. I might bring out the bubbles or allow the kids to take a long bath with new bath toys—whatever would give me some downtime, even as I kept my eye on them. At other times, we'd refuel together with a trip to the frozen yogurt café or a quick jaunt to the park or playground.

Today when I find myself depleted, I stop to take stock of what is going on in my mind. I place my worries in God's hands. Next I simplify my schedule. I plan a snack-style dinner, maybe crackers and cheese or fruit and toast, and break out the paper plates. I take a day off from regular commitments and plan to be still.

The next day, I again set aside my normal commitments so I can attack the most pressing, demanding tasks that are weighing me down. But I also plan some simple pleasures—making time to enjoy several cups of coffee or tea, squeezing in a fifteen-minute nap, watching a show, or reading a magazine. These activities give me the short break I know I need.

Obviously, times of disaster or hard-and-fast deadlines sometimes require our attention for extended periods. As long as there is an end to these demands, we can live like this temporarily. But refueling and refreshment are necessary to living well long term.

Managing our stress and our rest is a sign of living wisely. Refueling as a way to find joy, to create pleasure, and to celebrate life in the midst of all its demands fills our hearts with renewed hope. When we take the time to breathe, listen, and rest from the daily grind, we will slowly but surely begin to see miracles bubbling up in our lives.

Jesus' close friends, Lazarus and his sisters, Martha and Mary, often hosted the Lord in their home. In the Gospel of Luke, we read about one of those visits. Martha, frantically preparing that day's meal, asked Jesus to scold Mary because she was sitting at Jesus' feet rather than helping in the kitchen. Instead, Jesus kindly chided Martha. He knew that a "Martha heart," frenetically busy, would never see the miracles of God. "My dear Martha, you are worried and upset over all these details!" He told her, "There is only one thing worth being concerned about. Mary has discovered it, and it will not be taken away from her" (Luke 10:41-42, NLT).

Jesus wasn't admonishing Martha for doing her work. He was, however, concerned that she was too busy living in the whirlwind of her own making and trying to subsist on her own meek provisions. No wonder she seemed to have lost all hope and become a wretched nag. Jesus, God incarnate, was right in front of her, and her mind was so preoccupied that she wasn't even aware of His presence. Aren't we the same way?

I have learned a secret. My Prince Jesus comes to me at just the right time. As in the story "Sleeping Beauty," my "Prince" comes not when I am searching the horizon and pounding my fists. Instead, He comes when I am asleep, or at least when I am doing nothing but resting.

Resting in Him, choosing peace, and temporarily setting aside my responsibilities can be such grand medicine for my soul. After resting and investing in fun, my strength is renewed and all life's issues can be faced with grace.

As you seek to walk ever more closely with God, you may begin practicing still more spiritual disciplines that are modeled in the Scriptures. These include:

obedience: practicing doing what God tells you to do
stewardship: giving your time, money, talents, and skills to
    His purposes
meditating and fasting: taking special times away to allow
    God's voice to speak to you

There are so many resources that can guide you as you begin to practice these priorities. Just as athletes must learn the basics of their sport and then practice, practice, practice, so our spiritual lives require learning from God's Word about these means of drawing closer to Him and then investing in these disciplines.

✳

Own Your Part

A couple of years ago, I was teaching my fourth child to drive. When we started out, my daughter was overwhelmed by all she had to learn: getting the car out of park, keeping her foot on the brake, looking in her rearview mirror, and accelerating. "Mom, it is all too hard!" she told me. "I just can't get the hang of it." Yet recently after driving hundreds of hours, she quipped, "Sometimes driving comes so second nature to me that I have to remember to pay attention to what I am doing—because it is so effortless."

So it is in our spiritual walk with God. At first we may be unfamiliar with Scripture or prayer, but the more we invest time reading, praying, and pondering God, the more it becomes second nature to us.

1. Psalm 119:105 says, "Your word is a lamp to my feet and a light to my path." How can we know the ways of God in our lives if we do not have His words and voice informing our decisions? How disciplined are you in pursuing a deeper walk with God? Where do you need to grow?

2. How can you fit habits into the rhythms of your day so you will gain spiritual strength? Plan how you will fit reading and praying into your schedule as a daily investment. Without a plan, failure is assured. As you think about when to fit in quiet time, consider your own personality and time preference. Some women

are morning people, some afternoon, some evening. It does not matter when you spend time with God, but you are more likely to keep to a schedule if you figure out what would work best for you.

3. If you're not sure how to start reading your Bible regularly, you might consider using a book containing Scripture readings for each day. Two of my favorite daily devotions are listed below.

   • *Daily Light on the Daily Path*—This classic collection of Scripture readings for morning and evening is available in many published formats.

   • *Celtic Daily Prayer*—Published by the Northumbria Community, this book provides meditations, Scriptures, and spiritual quotations from godly people throughout the ages.

   Often, I choose a psalm a day to read, and I circle the attributes of God found in the passages.

4. Buy a journal in which to write down all the things for which you are grateful or a list of your prayer requests. Be sure to write in it at least once a week. Then it will become a history of God's faithfulness in your life.

Praying with You

Lord, we know You want to have conversation with us every day, because You are the One who created relationship. Please help us learn to be comfortable in Your presence, and teach us to become as close to You as You desire to be to us. We love You. Amen.

CHAPTER 9

LEARNING TO TAKE RISKS

Owning Your Faith

*It would seem that Our Lord finds our desires not too strong, but too weak.
We are half-hearted creatures, fooling about with drink and sex and ambition
when infinite joy is offered us, like an ignorant child who wants to go on
making mud pies in a slum because he cannot imagine what is meant by the
offer of a holiday at the sea. We are far too easily pleased.*
C. S. LEWIS, *THE WEIGHT OF GLORY*

*Without faith it is impossible to please Him, for he who comes to God must
believe that He is and that He is a rewarder of those who seek Him.*
HEBREWS 11:6

NEARLY SEVEN HUNDRED WOMEN had crammed into the hotel ball-room. I stood off to the side, butterflies flying uncontrollably through my stomach as I listened to female giggles and chattering, babies cooing, and women competing for a particular chair so they could sit near their friends. Though few of these women realized it, I knew this moment was a miracle. I was about to welcome guests to our ministry's first Mom Heart Conference, the result of my conviction that other moms must feel alone, as I often felt. I didn't think I was the only one who loved my children but struggled with isolation and boredom in the sometimes overwhelming details of daily life. I believed that, among like-minded women, there was a need for community as we strived to raise godly children without many people to teach us or to share our burden.

It had all begun several months before, in the fall of 1997, when I'd dropped with a sigh into the worn, slightly stained, overstuffed recliner in the living room. "This is just too hard for one woman to do on her own," I told Clay. "I don't feel up to all the tasks God has given me—children, work, ministry, marriage, finances, and keeping everyone fed. It's difficult holding it all together."

As my husband and I sat together in my mother-in-law's house, we talked one more time about our dreams for our ministry. We wanted to help inspire families to create a godly legacy for their children and to establish our own publishing house to produce materials that would be practical, user friendly, and inspiring. Three years had passed since we'd launched Whole Heart Ministries, and we had not yet received even one month of salary from all the work of building our dreams. And now, we were beginning to dream about starting a conference for women. One more risk!

We planned and schemed into the wee hours of that night. What would it cost to rent a hotel for hundreds of women? How many attendees did we think we would draw to the first of such events? How would we reach them with news of the conference?

Without any income, Clay and I came back to the question, Was it wise to take one more risk? Because I was still overwhelmed with the myriad details of my own life as a mother of young kids, I had to wonder, *Is this the right time?* But I felt in my heart that this kind of conference was just what I needed: inspiration without guilt, time with other women who shared my burdens, and an opportunity to renew my vision during a weekend of refreshment.

And so we prayed, "God, show us if this is on Your heart. Instruct our minds so we have the wisdom to know if You want us to host this conference, and give us agreement and unity of heart if this is what You want us to do." As we prayed, we both felt that God was giving us a green light. We felt He was telling us that He wanted us to take the risk to encourage moms in a culture that seemed to no longer value imagination and motherhood or leaving a legacy for godly children. So by faith we went ahead and rented hotel rooms. We also arranged for the meals and planned a conference schedule.

Critics seemed to be on every side. We call them "Job's friends"—those people who want to tell you what is wrong even though they are not living your life. "You need to just get a normal job!" (the mantra we had heard over and over since we began the adventure of starting our own ministry). "You are imposing on God to ask Him to bless this crazy idea." "You are taking too much risk, and the debt could ruin you for years to come." "You should not have rented such a big ballroom."

And yet we continued to move ahead. By the time we had finished planning and promoting the conference, we knew we would need 350 women to register to break even. We had no budget for advertising, so we gathered e-mail addresses and put up announcements in churches and bookstores. The Internet was relatively new back then, but we used it as best we could to promote the conference to groups of women, individuals, and churches. (Twitter and Facebook were not yet available.)

Two weeks before the conference, 350 women had registered! Ecstatic does not even begin to describe how amazed we were at the response. The kids had been praying their little hearts out with us. They whooped and jumped up and down in excitement when we told them we had reached that number. On the day of the conference, our hearts were filled with relief and praise for God as we saw 690 women squeezed into the ballroom. He had done far more than we could have imagined.

Foolishness or Faith?

What does God want from those of us who follow Him? Without faith, God tells us, it is impossible to please Him (see Hebrews 11:6).

But just what is faith? Is it pushing down feelings of doubt or squelching our questions and gutting it out as we repeat out loud, "I believe, I believe, I believe"? Or is it a vague fluttering in our hearts as we consider what we strongly wish would happen?

Faith, I've learned, is a mysterious process of following the voice of God, accompanied by hard work and wisdom. We step out in faith with engaged hearts as we pursue God's wisdom and ideals, which

He whispers to us as we seek Him. Clay and I had begun our marriage on the premise that God had a work for our family to do to bring His Kingdom to bear in real life. That certainty fueled the faith that enabled us to launch our family ministry and the Mom Heart Conferences. I believe God wants each of us to have the privilege of living by faith and watching Him work. It is His desire to respond personally to all of us who are His.

Faith is a mysterious process of following the voice of God, accompanied by hard work and wisdom.

Owning your faith means recognizing that your life belongs to God and then asking Him what work He wants to do through you. Each person and family has a story to tell. If you "seek first the Kingdom," you will leave your unique mark on your world and on the people who long to know more about Him. But you must pave the pathway by first stepping out, and then by following God's Word and His promptings by faith.

Faith Stealers

Satan hates it when we hold fast to God and wait on Him to provide for our needs. Jesus' disciple Peter knew this very well, especially after the night he denied knowing Jesus after Jesus had told Peter that Satan desired to sift him like wheat. As an older man, Peter warned other believers to "be of sober spirit, be on the alert. Your adversary, the devil, prowls around like a roaring lion, seeking someone to devour" (1 Peter 5:8).

The spiritual battle between God and Satan for the allegiance of men and women has been going on since the original Fall. Yet sometimes we fail to see that our faith is the test of our willingness to act on our allegiance to God.

Then there are the naysayers, those voices that tell us we are foolish for choosing to take a risk by living by faith. They criticize and try planting seeds of doubt and discouragement in our lives. When we identify them for what they are, we are able to prevent their negativity from reaching our hearts. If we are going to focus on pleasing God by faith, we must realize we will not always be able to please others.

Some of the deadliest faith stealers, however, come from within ourselves. When we choose to navigate our lives using fear, formula, or flesh, we set ourselves up for deep disappointment—and limit what God can do in and through us.

Fear

Fear says, "This isn't logical. This is not a safe decision. It is risky." When we listen to this voice, we tell ourselves, *I am going to make the safe decision. It would be foolish to put myself in circumstances I cannot control. I might fail. I can't see any way I can afford this on my own.*

Fear paralyzes us from moving forward. It stops faith in its tracks. Fear looks at the present dangers and refuses to trust in the future possibilities. Fear is often related to concerns about our performance or failure, and it quickly kills enthusiasm with the "facts." Yet God has gone to great lengths throughout history to show that we are not limited by human constraints.

Formula

Formula says, "What are the rules by which to live life? What is respected by the culture? What are the expectations of others? Just tell me the one right way to discipline children, or how I can make enough money to pay the bills, or the seven steps to having a good marriage, and I will follow that method."

Formula offers no room for individuality, unique personality, or circumstances. Formula puts everyone into the same box. Yet God rarely requires the same steps of faith from everyone; instead, He customizes His ways to every person's uniqueness.

Initially, formulas may make us comfortable because we feel more secure when we have rules to follow than when we have to live in the mystery of trusting God by faith, without all the answers immediately available.

Inevitably, though, formulas fail us. When that happens, we some-times attempt to use prayer as another formula. "Please get me out of this situation, and I come to You in the name of Jesus, by the blood He shed on the cross. Amen." We may then assume that God is obligated to answer our prayers because we said the words of the formula. And so we may trudge along in despair, wondering why God is so small and silent. I have been there. Many times. Yet this thinking puts God in our little box of expectations and doesn't allow for His sovereignty.

Flesh

Flesh is yet another means we use to try navigating life in our own strength. We tell ourselves, *If I try hard enough; if I work diligently; if I perform more perfectly and sin less; if I gut it out; if I give more money, attend more services, commit to more in ministry, then I will achieve God's will. I just need to do it by effort and willpower.*

Flesh is an attempt to live the Christian life by works and by manipulating circumstances in our own power. It doesn't require God's presence or blessing, and it attempts to do only what is logical or acceptable. Because it sees human possibility as the source of power, it limits God's infinite power to work. Flesh operates as if the spiritual life is all about personal effort and gutting it out.

Often, flesh shows up in our attempts to control, whether our circumstances, friends, family, children, or husbands. We want others to step in line so things happen according to our plans. But we don't have to live long to know that it is impossible to control life, and so losing control often leads to anger in those who expected to get good results by exerting force. Living the Christian life by the flesh is utterly exhausting and eventually wears us out.

Flesh, Formula, Fear, or Faith?

So many times I meet women who seem stuck in the mundane and the stress of life because they've become prisoners to their own thoughts and lack of faith. When in a rut, they tend to blame God. "Why has God done this to me? Why doesn't He answer my prayer?" It is an attitude that perpetuates spiritual blindness in a dark world that whispers, "God doesn't hear," and believes it.

Isolation, physical exhaustion, and overwork can cause us to feel desperate. When Elijah despaired of his life, God twice sent an angel to minister to him. Both times, the angel touched him, a sign of God's gentleness. Both times Elijah slept, and both times God provided food. In his case, physical refreshment helped lead to faith restoration.

Like Elijah, we often fall into despair. Depression is a common theme in the Psalms as well, and it is no indicator of spiritual weakness. We have justice built into our hearts, and disappointment in this fallen world can be severe and deep.

The reality of spiritual battle is sometimes subtle. Doubt fills our thoughts. Depression wraps its blanket of darkness around us when we are tired, weary from seeking to be faithful, and feeling alone.

We may be limited in our ability to believe in God because our heart vision is obscured by the voices, lies, and perspectives of the world that surrounds us. Sometimes we are discouraged to believe because God seems to be waiting too long to answer our prayers!

At such times our prayers express our longing to escape. We want out of our circumstances. When our prayers are more about His doing our will than our submitting to His, we have gotten off course.

If we are truly seeking God's will and ways in our lives, our focus must be on His Kingdom and the eternal soul work He wants to do in us. If we are willing to stay there, the difficult or desperate situation we are in might just be the place in which God wants to do a miracle.

When I fix my eyes on God as He really is, when I contemplate His larger purposes, and when I understand more about His power, greatness, endless love, and the scope of the blessings He has planned for me, my faith will stretch and grow. I want to live beyond my own abilities and tap into God's desire to provide for me according to His supernatural provision. God is waiting to abundantly provide for His children as they expect Him to manifest Himself according to His magnificent attributes.

That certainly was true for so many of the people we read about in the Bible. Over and over, we see how powerfully God responded to people of faith.

- Daniel entered a den of lions, by faith, and trusted His God to intervene. (Daniel 6)
- Moses stuck his toe in a vast, tempestuous sea with thousands of robust soldiers chasing behind him in chariots. He had faith that somehow God would save the motley crew of fathers, mothers, children, and infants in his care, not to mention all of their sheep and goats. (Exodus 14)
- Esther took the risk of advocating for the Jews, withstanding the anger of one of the wealthiest, most powerful men in Persia, not to mention that her husband, the king, could have had her banished and put to death. She invited both of these men to a feast by faith. (Esther 5)
- David, the shepherd boy, captivated God's heart because of his love and belief in his Creator. He vanquished a giant that had already demoralized the hearts of eight to ten thousand trained soldiers. And yet his words ring out through history: "You come to me with a sword, a spear, and a javelin, but I come to you in the name of the LORD of hosts." (1 Samuel 17:45)
- A bankrupt widow believed Elisha when he told her to take the one jar of oil that she had and pour it into as many empty vessels as she could find. The oil kept coming from her one jar until she had filled all the borrowed containers. As a result, she earned enough money to pay off her debt and support her family. (2 Kings 4)

- Rahab, a citizen of Jericho, hid Hebrew spies in her house, risking the wrath of her own people. (Joshua 2)

And lest we think that God no longer works in such miraculous ways, consider His care for those in modern times who have stepped out in faith, from Corrie ten Boom and her family, who hid Jews during the Holocaust, to Hudson Taylor, who dressed like a Chinese man so he could reach China with the gospel message.

These people came from a variety of backgrounds, and their stories are radically different. Each had to step out in faith in a different way, though they all found themselves

When I fix my eyes on God as He really is and contemplate His larger purposes, my faith will stretch and grow.

mired in the catastrophic demands of life in a fallen world. All of them acted from their belief that God would intervene.

As I reflect on my own life of faith, I recall the many times I have seen God provide so abundantly. He has blessed me in ways that are far beyond my own capacity to provide. Yet my decision to step out in faith was never announced with fanfare or balloons, but came in the mundane moments when I chose to engage my heart and believe God.

That was usually done in the quiet of my bedroom, alone with Him. Each time, He led me to believe that He would work faithfully in my circumstances to provide for a need, give an answer, or even supply the faith and long-suffering to meet a long-term challenge.

Often, the process began with my laying out a fear, burden, problem, or unjust situation before Him. Then, slowly, as I met God through Scripture reading and in prayer, He would gently ask me to give my burden to Him. Then as I sought His wisdom, He would impress upon me knowledge for the way to go forward (whether that meant forgiving someone, making a plan, extending love, contacting a person, or simply waiting on Him).

Often, taking a risk based on faith required me to decide to move in a new direction or take a new step:

- Accepting the challenge to go to Communist Eastern Europe as a young missionary. (After beginning with our team of six, that little ministry has now sent hundreds of full-time workers who have led countless thousands to Christ.)
- Having a child when I was forty-one, after three miscarriages, and despite hearing many times, "You are too old to have another baby." (That child is now in college.)
- Working with my husband for five years without a salary to start our publishing business. "Are you ever going to be responsible and get a job?" many voices asked. (We have published numerous books, which have been translated into eight languages, and hosted sixteen years of Mom Heart Conferences. We now dream of the next books to be written.)
- Homeschooling all of my children when everyone in my life thought I was crazy. (Now all four children reside in different cities, living their dreams and loving God—and by some miracle of grace, they love us, too!)

At times, walking in faith required me to stay put in difficult situations, waiting for God and believing that He was at work, even when I could not see it:

- Choosing not to spank a hard-to-handle child, which others advised. Instead, I gave him patience and grace until we eventually discovered he had severe OCD, ADHD, and a learning disorder.
- Watching another child battle severe health issues for thirteen years, going to many doctors and receiving many diagnoses with no results. In the end, her faith is deeper than that of most women I know because she wrestled with God and

found that He gave her hidden treasures in response to
her patience.

- Learning to tighten our belts and spend less as we lived through
years of unstable finances, believing that eventually our books,
conferences, and ministry would support our family. Truly
this built amazing character in the lives of my children, since
otherwise I could have spoiled them!
- Bearing years of criticism and judgment for living by our ideals
and waiting for God to show us that our labor was not in vain.
Now we are so thankful for the ways God worked through our
faith and brought so much fruit as we learned to obey His voice.

The steps of faith we took with our ministry validated our belief
that God created His children to invest in His work. We saw Him
bless our work beyond our own capacity so that His influence would
extend far beyond what we'd imagined. Like the widow in Elisha's
day, we sacrificed our little jar of oil to Him as a demonstration of our
belief. In God's hands, our little oil became an inexhaustible supply,
far exceeding our needs throughout the years. God's infinite power
made our finite offering a miracle.

In fact, it was when we took those first steps of faith and patiently
waited on God that He taught us profound spiritual truths. These are
a few of the lessons we learned along the way:

1. Strength and humility grow from exercising faith over
   many years.
2. God works differently in each person's life, so we cannot
   follow the pattern of other people's lives.
3. We do not always need what we think we do in order to
   be happy; rather, God's ways lead to contentment.

We learned many more lessons, but these three stand out in my memory.
Rather than asking God why He wasn't coming through for us in the

way we expected, we learned to pray, "Lord, we cannot control this situation, so we are giving it to You. We trust that You will show through our lives that You were indeed working and that You were willing to answer." Miracles, we discovered, come in the seemingly inconsequential moments when faith is engaged and practiced but no one else is looking.

A Legacy of Faith

God wants us to see Him as our personal and loving King who is willing to do miracles when we yield ourselves to Him. Living a spiritually exceptional life requires surrendering our limitations to Him.

The Lord desires to be fully engaged in the circumstances of your life, even when it means you must:

> admit a need, like not having enough food to stay alive, as the widow in Elisha's day did
>
> believe God for a marriage companion in a land where no one is suitable, as Isaac did
>
> trust God for victory in a battle where a giant is looming large, as David did
>
> walk into what seems to be a den of lions ready to engulf you, as Daniel did
>
> worship God in a difficult marriage, as Abigail did when she was Nabal's wife

No matter what our lives hold, God wants to work through the details and circumstances so that we will have a story of faith to tell throughout all of eternity.

If we obediently trust Him, wait for Him, and rest in the knowledge that He is good, even though we live in a fallen world, we will live to see His abundant blessing in His time.

> He redeems all.
> He restores all.
> He is the resurrection power.

When we live by faith, we accept that we may not understand everything until we are with God for eternity. That certainly was true for those faithful men and women whose stories are told in the Old Testament. The writer of Hebrews uses them as the backdrop to this eternal perspective on faith:

What more shall I say? I do not have time to tell about Gideon, Barak, Samson and Jephthah, about David and Samuel and the prophets, who through faith conquered kingdoms, administered justice, and gained what was promised; who shut the mouths of lions, quenched the fury of the flames, and escaped the edge of the sword; whose weakness was turned to strength; and who became powerful in battle and routed foreign armies. Women received back their dead, raised to life again. There were others who were tortured, refusing to be released so that they might gain an even better resurrection. Some faced jeers and flogging, and even chains and imprisonment. They were put to death by stoning; they were sawed in two; they were killed by the sword. They went about in sheepskins and goatskins, destitute, persecuted and mistreated—the world was not worthy of them. They wandered in deserts and mountains, living in caves and in holes in the ground. These were all commended for their faith.

HEBREWS 11:32-39, NIV

Each of us has our own story to tell in the greater tale of God's faithfulness throughout all kingdoms and times. Faith is a legacy you can pass on to your children as they observe the choices you make to believe God. Your life can become a pattern of hope for all the generations who will come after you.

We cannot sit on the sidelines of the world and expect to please

God. Either we engage in the battles by faith as His warriors, or we become Satan's prisoners of war, ensnared so that we are unable to do anything of eternal value, live as victims, and never enjoy the glory that comes from playing our part in God's story.

Own your faith. Take responsibility for the miracles God wants to do in and through your life. No one else can faithfully show the people He has entrusted into your care what it means to live by faith. No one else can accomplish the work He created you to do.

＊

Own Your Part

My son dreamed of God using him in Hollywood. After years of living as a starving artist and barely making ends meet because he would not accept roles that would compromise his faith, he poured his heart out to God. God spoke to him in his tiny apartment. "I want you to begin writing the kinds of scripts you think would become the kind of movies that would honor Me."

He stepped out in faith, wrote a script, raised money, and organized actors, and now his first film, *Confessions of a Prodigal Son*, is going to screen. He discovered that being a part of God's work in the world requires a heart of faith and then hard work and obedience.

1. What circumstances are you in right now that require you to give them to God, allow Him to work, and wait until He answers so that you can see His greatness above your own human vision?

2. What work or dreams has God placed on your heart to accomplish? What step of faith do you need to take?

3. What difficulty are you facing, and how will you be faithful to wait for God to work through the "lions of your life" or the

"giant" that is looming large? Will you wait for Him and worship Him in this place until you see the salvation of God?

Heroes are not those who do not feel fear or see the difficulty of their circumstances, but those who choose courage or action when in danger, fear, or need.

Praying with You
Dear God, we know You delight in rewarding the faith of Your children. It is Your way. Help us to be willing to look beyond the present realities of this world so that we can live to please You. Give us patience to wait to see Your personal miracles reserved uniquely for those who took the risk to believe. In Jesus' name we come. Amen.

CHAPTER 10

TENDING YOUR HEART AND INVESTING IN YOUR SOUL

Owning Your Emotional Health

The true beauty in a woman is reflected in her soul.
AUDREY HEPBURN, QUOTING SAM LEVENSON

Watch over your heart with all diligence,
For from it flow the springs of life. PROVERBS 4:23

A WISE WOMAN TAKES CARE OF HER EMOTIONAL HEALTH, her spiritual health, and her intellectual growth. That's why beautifying the corridors of your own soul will enable you to reflect a life of excellence. You cannot pour out what has not first been placed inside.

Investing in your soul life is the secret to becoming elegant, distinguished, gracious, refined, and spiritually captivating. But soul refining requires intentional planning and prioritizing. Women who grow more lovely with time have practiced pouring into themselves all that is excellent, wise, graceful, good, and true.

As my husband and I moved toward the celebration of thirty years of marriage, we dreamed together of a trip to England. Our mutual love for great literature, English mysteries, strong black English tea served in real china, bookstores, and our Celtic family heritage all seemed substantial reasons for us to take a trip to the United Kingdom.

We dreamed, planned, located tiny villages we planned to visit, and saved our pennies!

But life rudely interrupted our plans, and I spent our thirtieth anniversary bouncing over the rough roads of West Texas in a rental truck with my twenty-five-year-old son. We were returning from my mother's funeral and the dispersal of her worldly goods. Clay was laid up in bed with a ruptured disc, a calcified bone mass interwoven into his spinal column, while awaiting a very serious and intricate surgery. Our dream trip didn't happen.

Finally, two years later, Clay said, "Even if I am not able to travel that far, you should take the trip and explore all the places we dreamed about. You can come home with a full report. I know how much it means to you, and I want you to go, even if we can't go together!"

And so, providentially, a wonderful opportunity arose—and I found myself in the merry old country with my two oldest children.

There is a glory and grace in becoming older when your children-turned-adults shape and inspire new horizons in your life from their own vibrant souls. Flying to England for the occasion of celebrating the life and influence of C. S. Lewis had been the idea of my writer daughter, who had studied him at Oxford.

Sarah reflected, "All we have to do is save and do a little extra work, and we will have enough for our flight, hotels, and at least one formal English tea! This is our opportunity to be part of a historical occasion as a plaque commemorating the remarkable works of Lewis is placed in Westminster Abbey. One thousand people will be allowed to attend a free seminar given by outstanding speakers and lecturers who are experts on the writings of C. S. Lewis.

"The great cathedral will close to the public and be open just to those who gather to celebrate the influence Lewis has had through his writing. It is not an occasion that we, as writers, will want to miss. Just think of the thousand people we will be with who want to celebrate great ideas together!"

And so every month we saved money, frequent flyer miles, and hotel points from conferences, and planned and anticipated our fairy-tale trip. My own life, wearied from constant serving and teaching, had left me depleted, and so I eagerly anticipated our getaway. Joel, my composer son, decided he could not miss an occasion to live one more adventure-memory together, as was our custom, and joined us in London.

Soon after we had arrived, I pushed through crowds at twilight, my adrenaline rushing as I attempted to keep up with the long strides of my six-foot-five-inch son. He was leading us to a special surprise he'd orchestrated even before the event at Westminster Abbey.

Submerging into the crowded London subway, packed tightly against the breath and warmth of those standing next to me, I flashed smiling eyes at my two adult children who were leading me on this surprise adventure. Both winked back, acknowledging our mutual excitement.

This evening that Joel had planned was icing on the cake. It was meant to further civilize our hearts and minds, and he guided us through the crowds with eagerness, anticipating what was ahead. As we exited the dark hall of the crowded subway, the sparkling lights from hundreds of windows lining the circular perimeter of Royal Albert Hall filled the skyline.

"A concert of great proportions will be played tonight, and I secured some of the last tickets available," he said, beaming. "Brahms's Requiem will be played amidst a choir of hundreds of voices accompanying the London Philharmonic."

Lights dimmed and haunting melodies tiptoed gently into every corner of my soul, overtaking thoughts and guiding my heart to feel the breathtaking anguish and longing a child has for a mother lost forever through death. A hundred voices joined in the hymn of memorial, written to mark and remember the preciousness of a loved one who had departed far too soon. Familiar and favorite passages of Scripture were sung and blended into swells of the hauntingly moving music.

I wasn't prepared for how touched I would be by the glory of such music. Tears spilled down my cheeks as my soul began to find rest in the sweeping melodies. I remember thinking, *How is it possible this has been in existence my whole life and I have never heard it before?*

Taking in its beauty, I stored the memory as a reflection of what I wanted to express through my own life. Gratitude and thankfulness filled my heart as confirmation that taking a vacation, saving our money, and risking to be here had been a great investment that I had needed to refresh myself in a weary season. We were indeed made for beauty, and the loveliness of the evening filled me with hope and courage to live a better life.

A few days later, we headed to Westminster Abbey for the celebration of Lewis's life and work. The Abbey never disappoints our expectations of grandeur. As we entered, we were greeted by excited whispers and swishing footsteps echoing off the stone floor, as over one thousand people from all parts of the world gathered to celebrate C. S. Lewis, the provocative professor and ale-drinking, orphan-protecting story weaver so many had come to love. An artisan of words, he had inspired readers to love God, while thrilling us to our tiptoes with a renewed perception for living life well. The ornate cathedral, where kings and queens had been crowned, royal weddings performed, and over three thousand famous writers, musicians, soldiers, and statesmen commemorated, was a sort of archetype for what will happen when people from all centuries gather with Jesus at the final banquet He prepares for us.

During the service, C. S. Lewis's own voice, captured in a rare recording, boomed out through the hall. A final reading from *The Last Battle* reminded each of us to draw "further up and further in" to Aslan, the great lion who depicts our glorious Savior.

Soaking in the reality that Lewis's greatness came from living a life of integrity in his faith fed my desire to live so that those behind me could see the palpable reality of God.

Our exceptional, once-in-a-lifetime adventure fed my soul for months. The ideas worth pondering had stimulated my thinking. The glorious music gave pleasure and renewed my own scope of worship. Strong tea, cakes, and scones shared amidst formal clothes, civilized conversation, and soft music had created a sense that for a moment my children and I were royalty, celebrating life together.

Trips like this one are not a normal part of my life, and yet I have learned that creating memories, planning times of grand celebration, and placing myself in the pathways of great people fill and enrich my soul, so that when others draw from me, they find interest, insight, fun, and wisdom.

"He who walks with wise men will be wise" (Proverbs 13:20) is a mantra my children have heard me repeat their whole lives.

These memories will be stored forever on the shelves of my heart for pondering and using. If I were able to see what lined the shelves of your mind and soul, what would I find there? How have you owned the stewardship of spending time with inspiring people and feeding on life-giving ideas, profound books, and beautiful art or music so that grace overflows from within you?

Heart, Mind, and Soul Restoration

Life is draining, every moment, all the time. We have bills to pay, work to do, meals to make, people to care for, tasks to complete—and then we must repeat these tasks again and again.

When we are constantly emptying our hearts, minds, and souls, it is essential that we take responsibility to keep filling them up. What we feed our inner beings will determine what we can give to those in our spheres of influence. What we have stored, cherished, and valued in our lives is reflective of our true selves.

Our hearts and souls are vessels to hold all that we deem valuable. If loveliness of values, greatness of thoughts, and civility of life are treasured there, the people who come into our presence will draw beauty from our lives.

One of the most important lessons I learned in my midforties was that I needed to take responsibility for my own education, for filling my soul and mind with excellence and inspiration, and for caring for my physical well-being so that I would maintain emotional, spiritual, and physical health.

God built such life-giving beauty into the universe. The very first verse of the Bible says, "In the beginning God created . . ."

Artist, crafter of all things beautiful in the universe, God planned His works of art for our pleasure and admiration. He provided us with senses—the ability to smell, touch, hear, see—as evidence of His desire for us to take pleasure in the world He made.

Some Christians are afraid to enjoy life, or at least to admit out loud that pleasure is spiritual. Measuring the value of their worship by their good deeds, sacrifice, and service, they often overestimate the strength of their spiritual lives.

It is possible that God would disagree with their assessments. He has planted beauty and splendor in every space, every corner of the universe. God is an artist at heart, and His desire to delight us is evident throughout the created cosmos. It is designed to elicit our worship.

An artist is greatly praised when his admirers enjoy and approve the excellence of his creative works. When we take time to celebrate what is truly good and enjoy all that our heavenly Father has made for our pleasure, we honor Him. A thankful heart that recognizes the blessing of a meal well made, a song magnificently composed, a garden well planted, or a massage skillfully given is a heart that delights in the goodness of God and shares in His joy. As people celebrate fun, beauty, creativity, and feasting, God opens many hearts so they want to know Him who is vastly beyond our limited imaginations.

God is an artist at heart, and His desire to delight us is evident throughout the created cosmos.

Jesus ushered in His ministry by making the most delectable wine at a wedding celebration. His return will be marked with a great feast of unimaginable delicacies of sweet and savory cuisine, prepared for those who have faithfully served Him. His very nature is to celebrate and experience that which is marvelous in design.

God has filled the world with potential pleasures. We glory in His creation when we enjoy what He has made. God loves for us to be happy, to celebrate life, and to thank Him for being the source of our fulfillment.

If we wish to live out the best virtues of life, we must feed our minds, hearts, and souls upon all that is virtuous. Our souls reflect our true selves. What we have fed upon will be reflected through the ways we live in relationship to people and to the culture at large.

Philippians 4:8 gives us a list of virtuous ideals upon which to focus our spiritual and mental appetites: "Whatever is true, whatever is honorable, whatever is right, whatever is pure, whatever is lovely, whatever is of good repute, if there is any excellence and if anything worthy of praise, dwell on these things."

I meet very few women who seem exemplary of character and soul, whose lives challenge me to be more excellent. I'm not talking about perfect performance in life but about devotion and contagious passion—not behavior, but heart. Women who know their God should be mirror reflections of His beauty, vibrant character, generous love, and wisdom. But to reflect such attributes, we must invest time and thought in what our minds and hearts are becoming.

The Consequence of Death

Thousands of years in a world separated from the life of God have replaced what was designed to be beautiful with cynicism, immorality, technical advancement, utilitarian values, and materialism. We value efficiency over artistic expression and often exist in an impersonal culture separated from family and friends. As a result, we have diminished the value of life as God created it.

If ugliness, anger, coarseness of spirit, resentment, criticism, and darkness permeate the moments of our existence, then our souls will reflect the darkness hiding and residing in our hearts.

Scripture tells us to guard our hearts because they hold the very wellsprings of our lives (see Proverbs 4:23). Guarding implies an action taken to protect or to shield from harm. Protecting the borders of our hearts from all that is ugly or that would destroy faith or diminish love is a proactive commitment that must be made if we desire to pour out beauty instead of ugliness.

Owning the boundaries of what fills our hearts and minds must be a commitment that we honor every day. When we constantly pour out our energy, time, service, and work for the sake of others, we must realize our need to fill back up so we can maintain our spiritual vibrancy, hope, and emotional health.

Developing Soul-Filling Habits

Pleasure

God has filled the world with potential pleasures. We glory in His creation when we enjoy what He has made. God loves for us to be happy, to celebrate life, and to thank Him for being the source of our fulfillment.

Nature

For many years, I lived in very poor countries, where food was scarce and life was barren. Often when out walking, I would observe tall, ugly, concrete apartment buildings with laundry hanging on balconies and walls gray from the smog and industrial waste in the air. Yet always in the midst of hundreds of balconies, there would be an exception— a balcony with window boxes filled with red, pink, and coral geraniums that set the apartment apart from hundreds of others. I always imagined that those who dwelled there had souls alive, and I wished I could know them.

Walking under the stars, cherishing fields of flowers, being carried by a salty wave in the ocean, petting the soft fur of a puppy and reveling in its humor, watching storm clouds hover over snowcapped mountains— all are experiences that soothe our weary bodies and bring refreshment.

In a world of technology, we often forget to live in what is real. I walk out every day in the fresh air, breathing in the color and the calm that God has placed in my life. Having no curtains on my bedroom windows offers me the sweep of pinks and purples in a morning sunrise or the concert of falling snow pecking my windows in winter.

But to enjoy nature, I must make myself pay attention to what surrounds me daily and take time to enjoy and admire the beauty God has granted us through what He has made.

The Art of Life

Recently while I was speaking at a conference in a large hotel, a friend tapped on my door and walked in. Finding me sitting on a couch, with lyrical music coming from a small speaker and a candle wrapped in a multicolored scarf fluttering on the coffee table, she asked, "Are you for real? Do you always do this?" I'd also set out a tiny bowl of salted almonds, dried cherries, and pieces of dark chocolate and poured her steaming-hot, fragrant tea into a real china cup. I had created an atmosphere of pleasure, which now invited her into my world.

Traveling sometimes twenty-five weekends a year has become the norm for my life as a speaker, teacher, and missionary. This lifestyle constantly depletes rather than fills. Second-rate, unhealthy food, sterile environments, and exhausting travel all take their toll. Long ago, I learned to create my own home atmosphere wherever I journeyed, to keep my body more rested and refueled amidst the limitations that my work life held. The reality is, each soul creates an atmosphere based on what it cherishes.

Even when our children traveled with us regularly, we gave each of them their own travel briefcases with their names embroidered across the top. They were filled with music and story cassettes, LEGOs, small snacks, picture books, puzzle books, paper airplane kits, magazines, bubbles, and small surprises to inspire them along the route. We also brought nuts, water bottles, apples, grapes, carrots, packets of hummus and whole grain cereal, and gluten-free crackers for them to munch on in hotel rooms. And of course, we played their favorite soothing music at bedtime.

Seeking to fill our souls along the way, regardless of the limitations of our lives, requires planning and creativity. For many years, I did not understand this principle of wisdom. A doctor once said to me, "You can kill yourself at an early age if you want to, but you need to change some things if you want to thrive."

I learned to say no to some great opportunities that would ultimately be too taxing. But planning to travel with more grace and to take some days of pleasure and rest amidst my trips helped transform a deficit into a surplus. The creativity of crafting a better life was actually quite fulfilling.

Seeking to refill your soul along the way requires planning and creativity.

Music

Music is a favorite relaxation of mine and plays in our home morning, noon, and night. Music actually improves the ability to concentrate, lowers blood pressure, and just brings a whole lot of fun. Celtic, classical, contemporary, acoustic, jazz, and rock are all genres that are part of the musical appetite in our home. We choose the mood of the music based on the occasion. We also sometimes fit concerts featuring favorite artists or favorite pieces into our schedule.

Feasting

Eating is so much fun—not to mention something our bodies must do every day to keep alive. Feasting is eating with the celebration of life and community in mind. An unprecedented variety of food and tastes is available to us since we have the ability to transport food from all over the world to local stores.

Organic, fresh, homemade, savory international cuisine is my preference. Our family adopted many comfort foods as favorites, too.

Each evening in our home, whether we had a bowl of oatmeal or a large roasted turkey with all the trimmings, we lit candles, put on a variety of our favorite melodies, and made eating together an event. Great discussions, heartfelt stories, and close memories were cultivated from this daily habit.

Building Mental Muscle

Love God with all of your mind is part of the greatest commandment. God wants to be honored in our thoughts, our education, our theology, and our work. When we take seriously the stewardship of investing in truth; honesty; goodness; purity; and virtuous, demanding academics as a part of our worship of God, we will grow amazingly strong in our ability to think with clarity.

Our minds have such incredible potential, and yet like any muscle, they must be exercised in order to grow strong. Building mental strength comes from developing a habit of reading every day, a stewardship that exposes our minds to great thinkers and writers. Reading is the primary way our brains take in ideas, build paths, develop connected thoughts, and expand our vocabularies and nuances of knowledge.

Exposing yourself to people wiser than you will make you wise. Read those whose writing is profound in their fields, and consider trying one or more of these ideas:

- Invest in reading and memorizing passages from the Bible every day.
- Read biographies of heroic people to be inspired.
- Read great stories for pleasure, which will fill your personal imagination with courage and healthy sentiments. Stories are one of the best sources of hope, entertainment, and inspiration.
- Collect classic children's literature to become engaged in the age-old narrative of good triumphing over evil. Reading these aloud to your children will form your souls on mutual stories

and will provide a foundation of inspiration, moral excellence, and family closeness.

- Read spiritual classics every day, and feed your soul on deep devotional concepts that will stretch your understanding of spirituality or theology.

Fill your mind with a healthy diet of great thoughts, and your mind will grow strong by what you have fed it. Most great leaders, teachers, and people in influential positions are avid readers. Even starting to be faithful to this habit a little bit at a time will greatly improve your outlook on life. Investment in truth brings inspiration and lasts your whole life.

Your personality and interests play a role in what will bring your soul contentment. Evaluate who you are and the things that truly fill your emotional cup. Enriching your soul and guarding your heart are elegant works of life-art. Endless possibilities exist of ways you can invest in joy, pleasure, and excellence and make them the hidden resources of your life. When you learn to take responsibility for your own well-being, you will produce a harvest of influence and grace in every other area that is influenced by your heart health.

You and I shall answer to God for what we fed our minds, how we treated our bodies, and what we celebrated in life. May the fires of our souls burn brighter with each year.

✳

Own Your Part

Recently I was reminded that tending your heart doesn't have to be complicated. Joy and I were the only two at home, so we decided to jump in the car and have dinner at a new café we'd heard about. After splitting a burger, we took a walk down a nearby block lined with Victorian homes. We had such fun waving to families eating dinner or swinging on their front porches. As we breathed in the cool night air, we shared some of the thoughts and dreams that had been on our minds.

Simple moments like these are life giving. In fact, they seem to line up with Jesus' desire to give His followers joy and peace in the midst of their ordinary lives. While speaking to a crowd, Jesus offered this invitation: "Come to Me, all who are weary and heavy-laden, and I will give you rest. Take My yoke upon you and learn from Me, for I am gentle and humble in heart, and you will find rest for your souls" (Matthew 11:28-29). That invitation still stands. Will you take it?

1. Nature, music, books, healthy foods, conversation with good friends—each of these is a good gift from God that can help restore your soul. Which one appeals to you most? How might you incorporate that gift into your schedule this week?

2. Another way to tend to your soul is to focus on the "art of life." What would that look like in your own life and home?

3. How might you begin to fill your mind with great thoughts?

Praying with You

Lord Jesus, we praise You because You came to restore life to our bodies, souls, and minds. Help us to seek You today in the midst of all the good gifts You have given us, and may we be refreshed by Your Word, Your creation, and all that we take in through our senses. And then, O Lord, help us to become life givers within our homes, neighborhoods, and churches, for Your glory. Amen.

CHAPTER 11

CHOOSING TO OVERCOME: MOVING BEYOND HURT

Owning Your Response to Others

As long as we continue to live as if we are what we do, what we have, and what other people think about us, we will remain filled with judgments, opinions, evaluations, and condemnations. We will remain addicted to putting people and things in their "right" place. HENRI J. M. NOUWEN

Do not judge so that you will not be judged. For in the way you judge, you will be judged; and by your standard of measure, it will be measured to you. MATTHEW 7:1-2

IRPS: IR-RATIONAL PEOPLE (PLURAL)

Clay and I came up with this acronym years ago after a number of surprise encounters with people—some who didn't even know us well—who suddenly lashed out in anger or felt the freedom to criticize or create conflict out of the clear blue sky. We called such people, who divide and discourage, the "IRPS" in our lives.

The surprise for me as a young, naive believer was that the biggest hurts I would experience would come from other Christians. The sting of mean-spirited words, hatefulness, criticism, and judgment from people we encountered in ministry, at church, in Bible studies, and through our blogs sometimes pushed me into depression or devastating dark-night-of-the-soul experiences. I've also seen many colleagues lose their heart to stay in Christian ministry because of the ways they have been treated by other believers who felt they had a right to be caustic and derisive.

Had I known as a young Christian that believers could be exceptionally harsh and cruel and that the enemy would try to use them to discourage me from living a life of faith, I might not have been so devastated the first few times I experienced condemnation. And yet now I am better able to handle conflict because of the wisdom I've gained from battles fought.

Anger and rejection hurt all of us deeply, but while we might expect those who do not know Christ to be unloving, the unjust criticism from other Christians often takes us by surprise. We expect them to be loving, grace giving, and accepting, just as Jesus is and as He admonishes us to be. Owning your commitment to overcome such wounds requires perspective, insight, and fortitude! Part of being an effective warrior for Christ in this fallen world is understanding the ways the enemy will seek to destroy us.

Hurt may come at the hands of your family, those in your inner circle at church, a Christian leader, someone you thought was your best friend—from any number of places. But these wounds do not characterize you unless you allow them to define your view of God and keep you down and discouraged. To live a vibrant Christian life, you must be prepared to be shot at by those who are supposedly on your side. To stay resilient in your faith, to "overcome evil with good" (Romans 12:21), you cannot stay bitter but must move beyond the hurt to the wholeness Christ offers.

Through the Eyes of Grace

Not long ago, I attended a weeklong conference for educational leaders, which drew people from every kind of spiritual underpinning: atheists, agnostics, and a handful of (very vocal) evangelical Christians, as well as people who just didn't care or know much about faith.

I eventually developed a couple of friendships with people whose hotel rooms were near my own. One fifty-year-old woman was especially friendly and outgoing, so we began attending many conference sessions together.

As we found out a little more about each other with each passing day, I noticed that my new friend seemed to be getting quieter and a little more reserved. On the fourth day, she said, "Sally, I think if you really knew what I was like, you would be ashamed of me and ashamed to be seen with me. But I feel like I need to be honest with you. Actually, I am ashamed of myself, but I can't change my past."

I told her there was nothing she could do that would possibly change my opinion of her.

"I just have to tell you," she said. "I have been married and divorced three times, and I am living with a new boyfriend now. I walk around with guilt hanging around my heart because I have been such a failure at love."

Looking into her eyes, I gently responded, "What I see is a loving woman. You sparkle everywhere you go. You have befriended me and made me feel more comfortable at this conference than anyone else. You are interesting to talk to, and you make me evaluate my own ideas. You have a sense of responsibility and help others; you show up on time and are very professional in your behavior. And most of all, what I see is a thoughtful, encouraging friend!"

Tears sprang up in her eyes. "So you still want to be my friend?"

"Of course I do; you are a gift to me!"

Her words still weighed on my heart when I visited the hotel gift shop later that day. I found a beautiful candle that I thought might encourage my friend. I left it for her at the front desk, along with a card on which I'd written, "I am so grateful I met you. Your friendship has brought me light this week."

Late that night, as my lids drooped in sleepiness after a long day, I heard a slight shuffle as a note was slipped under my hotel room door.

Curious, I dragged myself out of bed and opened the envelope. As I began reading, my weariness was replaced with joy. "I have never received such an unexpected gift like this before. I have never felt loved before by someone who knew my past. I am changed forever. Thank you, thank you for accepting me and still liking who I am.

I will no longer define myself by my past, but by the love and affirmation I have felt in the words you spoke into my life."

When we love others, we are simply reflecting the undeserved grace that we have received. Over and over in Scripture, we see God's love coming to others before they were even looking for it, whether the Samaritan woman; the woman caught in adultery; Zacchaeus, the tax collector; or the lepers.

Many passages recount God's abundant provision of love for us:

God shows his love for us in that while we were still sinners, Christ died for us. ROMANS 5:8, ESV

God so loved the world, that he gave his only Son, that whoever believes in him should not perish but have eternal life. JOHN 3:16, ESV

See what kind of love the Father has given to us, that we should be called children of God; and so we are.
1 JOHN 3:1, ESV

Every person was born to know the gracious, undeserved love of our Creator God. People need to know they are loved before they can even begin to comprehend or understand the love of God and the sacrifice He made to forgive their sins. And so my new friend has been inching toward God's love

> *When we love others, we are simply reflecting the undeserved grace that we have received.*

as she better understands that she was created to know Him. I believe that only the loved can love and only the found can find others. We love others so they can then understand what His love is like.

Unfortunately, the story does not end here. It takes a turn for the worse.

After I shared this story with a Christian friend, she said, "Sally,

I am shocked at you. You need to correct that woman's behavior and tell her she has done wrong in the eyes of God. You should have let her know that you did not approve of her actions. You are not being true to doctrine. I can't believe you treated her as though she was okay. I thought you were more conservative in your views of the Bible!"

My heart broke once again. Actually, this encounter was one of the milder conflicts I've had with other Christians; there are many more that almost devastated my faith. I have known too many believers who are more concerned with their doctrine than they are with Jesus. Many talk more about their philosophy and their boxes of faith than they talk about Jesus—His heart, His teachings, His sacrifice, His compassion, and His call to send us into the world to show His love to others.

It is easy to hyperfocus on doctrine and laws of righteousness and then leave Jesus outside when conflict arises. Often, the most legalistic and rules-driven believers are the quickest to sting others.

Living beyond Your Boxes

Because I work in ministry, I am surrounded by a variety of Christians who define themselves and their faith by their labels: Reformed, charismatic, egalitarian, complementarian, Spirit-filled, liturgical, Arminian, Baptist, Catholic, fundamentalist, and progressive, to name just a few.

These words are familiar to those of us who spend lots of time in the Christian subculture, yet they are totally foreign to many outside the church. Of course, I believe that each of us must grow in maturity and come to better understand the tenets of our faith. Yet all of us—no matter how long ago we came to faith—are called to be ambassadors, light bearers, and lovers first of all.

Interestingly, people outside the evangelical circles do not know or understand our labels; instead, they read our lives. People most often come to understand the redeeming love of Christ when they see us living with integrity, sacrificing our personal time, loving unconditionally, giving money generously, and reaching out with compassion.

Jesus said there is one simple way that people will know we are His disciples. It is not by the rules we keep, the church buildings where we worship, the clothes we wear, the movies we watch, or the formulas we keep. He said, "By this all men will know that you are My disciples, *if* you have love for one another" (John 13:35, italics added).

One little word profoundly influences the magnitude of Jesus' statement: *if.* If we have love for one another, they will know our love. People will not truly know we are His disciples unless we have love for one another.

People notice if we have love because the world does not naturally love well. Yet all of us long to be loved—especially when we do not deserve it. That's why the boxes or "theological underpinnings" that uniquely define various groups of Christians generally come later to a new believer.

The world and nonbelievers evaluate or judge us by how we behave, how well we love, how hard we work, how willing we are to listen, and not by the particular nuances of our tenets of faith. This principle is also true with children. Our children learn to read our lives, and they long for our love before they believe our doctrines.

> **People notice if we have love because the world does not naturally love well.**

You must first own your testimony as a transformed servant and lover of Christ in order to live a life of true influence in a world lost to the love of God. It is not your labels that will draw others to Him—it is the way He is lived out generously through the moments and relationships of your life.

No Pointing Fingers

Many believers today often exchange harsh words and "judgmentalism" on the Internet. Yet I frequently wonder why Christians so often spew hatred toward those who do not know Christ. Why should we expect those who do not know or value Scripture to behave in a biblical way? Jesus came to sacrifice His life because all of us were broken. And without Him we are utterly helpless. Yet legalism, self-righteousness, and judgment have been the practices of religious leaders since Jesus' day.

Because of their obsession with the rules and laws that they depended on for their salvation, the Pharisees and Sadducees, who were the ruling parties of the Temple and Jewish spiritual life, did not even recognize the Son of God. They cherished their laws so much that they had lost sight of their love for God.

Jesus, on the other hand, often hung around with tax collectors and other sinners, eating and associating with them so He could show them God's love. After all, you eat with someone because you desire to build a closer friendship, to get to know that person, to open pathways of conversation. Jesus was indeed seeking to befriend "sinners."

But the Pharisees, who measured their holiness by external cleanliness—the actions people could observe on the outside—would never openly associate with someone who was questionable in their society. We read several accounts in the Bible of religious leaders trying to trap Jesus because they wanted to condemn Him.

> As Jesus was reclining at the table in the house, behold, many tax collectors and sinners came and were dining with Jesus and His disciples.
>
> When the Pharisees saw this, they said to His disciples, "Why is your Teacher eating with the tax collectors and sinners?"
>
> But when Jesus heard this, He said, "It is not those who are healthy who need a physician, but those who are sick.
>
> But go and learn what this means: 'I desire compassion, and not sacrifice,' for I did not come to call the righteous, but sinners." MATTHEW 9:10-13

I find it interesting that the Pharisees were not brave enough to confront Jesus directly. So they cast doubt about Him in the eyes of the disciples, Jesus' inner circle, by questioning His behavior. Basically, they were saying, "Why is your teacher hanging around with the untouchables—the people whose values are different from ours, the ones who have done bad things, the ones we would be embarrassed to associate with?"

Jesus is God, and He is aware of everything. He heard their whisperings and responded directly to their criticism. He implied that He was a physician sent to heal those who knew they were ill. But then the most penetrating issue came to the forefront as He admonished these deceitful men, "Learn what this means: 'I desire compassion, and not sacrifice'" (9:13).

Jesus was referring to a verse from the Old Testament that the Pharisees would have known well: "I want you to show love, not offer sacrifices. I want you to know me more than I want burnt offerings" (Hosea 6:6, NLT).

How His words must have burned in the hearts of these selfish, critical men. They obviously were more concerned about sacrifices, law, and external justice than they were about loving the lost.

These leaders were known by the crowd of "tax collectors and sinners" as hypocritical men who cared nothing for them. They were so concerned about their precious "boxes" that they could not see the great need in the hearts of the very people they were condemning.

Paul, a former Pharisee, was an avid student of the Torah, or the Old Testament Law. He must have seen the same problem among those in his ministry. In the book of Romans, he unifies the laws of righteousness with the law of love and explains what is most important.

> *Owe nothing to anyone except to love one another; for he who loves his neighbor has fulfilled the law.* For this, "You shall not commit adultery, You shall not murder, You shall not steal, You shall not covet," and if there is any other commandment,

it is summed up in this saying, "You shall love your neighbor as yourself." Love does no wrong to a neighbor; therefore love is the fulfillment of the law.

ROMANS 13:8-10, ITALICS ADDED

Let me repeat this amazing phrase: "Owe nothing to anyone except to love one another; for he who loves his neighbor has fulfilled the law."

Radical words indeed! We often long to justify our behavior, to have our own way, to criticize others for their sinful behavior, and to point fingers, in spite of the fact that we ourselves are sinful and self-ish. Jesus gave and gave His unconditional love, and He admonished us to love one another, but we seem to be thick skulled or slow to learn. Often, it seems to me, we try applying countless measures of proper Christian conduct except for loving one another.

I am sometimes embarrassed at the harshness and division that Christians create by spewing anger and being so publicly hateful and full of rage toward non-Christians who do not agree with their Christian principles. We should never expect the world to behave according to our morality, our standards of holiness, or our wisdom. Jesus would still call us to "owe them our love" to fulfill the law.

Define Yourself by Jesus, Not by Religious Rules

According to Hebrews 1:3, Jesus is "the radiance of [God's] glory and the exact representation of His nature, and upholds all things by the word of His power." In other words, when you see Jesus, you see God Himself, living in the flesh. Jesus embodies love, mercy, justice, holiness—all the attributes of God. When we ponder Jesus, we are pondering God and the way He would have us live.

Consequently, as I seek to know God by emulating Jesus, I will begin to acquire His ways, thoughts, and values for myself. When others interact with me, they should be encountering Jesus in and through my flesh. Hearing His words and observing His humility, servant heart, self-sacrifice, purposes, and truth should be the focus of my life. I make the Bible my study, but I have made the life of Jesus my meditation, the center of my own Christianity. Jesus' life is a living, soul-breathing story of God's complete grace encompassing the lost.

To look at Jesus is to see and behold God Himself. Jesus held a picnic and satisfied the hunger of thousands of people several times— He didn't just talk about truth; He satiated the hunger of rumbling stomachs. Jesus touched the untouchables—He touched prostitutes, lepers, the sick, and the dying with tenderness and love. He held children on His knee as He laughed with them and loved them.

Jesus was not afraid to rage at the religious leaders who showed off their legalism and performance but were not compassionate. He celebrated and drank wine at a wedding, cooked fish on the beach, and validated women for their service and tender love of Himself.

Jesus told unforgettable stories and preached epic sermons; He fed and celebrated with His own disciples. He comforted the sad, healed the brokenhearted, and inspired the vigorous young men around Him to live for a Kingdom that would never end. In His every waking hour He modeled the vast love, compassion, holiness, beauty, and servant leadership that express the very heart of God.

Jesus is not just a thought to be understood, a verse to be memorized, but a living, breathing, vibrant, loving, personal God who lives and breathes among us. He is the Way, and He is with us along the way.

The life and reality of a God who came to love, serve, and redeem is what my children, friends, neighbors, and husband long for in their hearts. They were made for a God who is more interesting, more diverse, and more challenging than any human being they will ever meet. For this reason, I seek to reflect Him, not just in my words but also in the way I take care to prepare my home as He prepared the first garden. I want to love as He loved and serve as He served.

People do not long for a philosophy; they long for relationship and to belong to something bigger than themselves. But I can only give to others what I have found to be true in my own life as I ponder Jesus' stories and see His transcendence through nature. I live from a soul fully engaged in Him after learning to love Him and better understand Him in my own quiet time.

The joy of life, which is contagious, comes from being in Christ's presence and enjoying Him. In one of his psalms, David reflects on God's love, saying, "In Your presence is fullness of joy; in Your right hand there are pleasures forever" (Psalm 16:11). Is that our experience? Do we believe this? Do we live it?

Learning to Move On

Though we may strive to emulate Jesus by loving others well, we've all been stung by the uncaring words or snide remarks of other people. I do not want to make light of the deep and abiding hurt you may have felt because of the anger, rejection, or scar-shaping relationships you've had with others, especially believers.

Yet I have learned through so many experiences that God heals me best when I am willing to move beyond the offense. It doesn't mean that the hurt won't bubble up throughout life, as sad experiences will always be sad. Moving beyond these circumstances so we don't allow them to immobilize us is part of the healing process. In addition, my heart of compassion and my desire to give grace to others have deepened and grown because of the injustices I have experienced.

The lessons I've learned from painful experiences and from spending time at Jesus' feet have also led me to some life-giving principles that reflect God's heart:

- Love when those in your life have failed you. As a choice of your will, love others who do not show compassion as Jesus did.

  Above all, keep loving one another earnestly, since love covers a multitude of sins. I PETER 4:8, ESV

- Don't react in kind to those who are unloving. Remember the testimony of Jesus at the Cross. I have learned that eventually those who are unjust or unloving are dealt with by Jesus. Bitterness will kill your soul.

> He did not retaliate when he was insulted,
>   nor threaten revenge when he suffered.
> He left his case in the hands of God,
>   who always judges fairly.
>
> I PETER 2:23, NLT

Remember how foolish and ugly our Christian testimony has become in this culture because of hateful, angry, judgmental public displays toward nonbelievers. Then decide not to partake in such demeaning displays.

- Practice forgiving as a choice of your will. Remember that forgiveness is not a feeling, but an action of your will. But remember, you cannot make another person be mature in his or her relationship toward you. You can only be mature yourself.

> Peter came and said to Him, "Lord, how often shall my brother sin against me and I forgive him? Up to seven times?" Jesus said to him, "I do not say to you, up to seven times, but up to seventy times seven."
>
> MATTHEW 18:21-22

- Practice saying words of love to those who need to hear them.

> The LORD appeared to him from afar, saying,
> "I have loved you with an everlasting love;
> Therefore I have drawn you with lovingkindness."
>
> JEREMIAH 31:3

- Establish love as the priority of your life, valuing it as Jesus did.

  [Jesus said,] "I have made Your name known to them,
  and will make it known, so that the love with which
  You loved Me may be in them, and I in them."
  JOHN 17:26

- Be discerning when entrusting yourself to others. Recognize that many fools (including immature Christians who lack perspective) will seek to draw you away from what is right. Love does not require you to be yoked to those who would pull you away from the heart of God. Proverbs is filled with admonitions to avoid immature and unwise fools.

  Do not answer a fool according to his folly,
  Or you will also be like him.
  PROVERBS 26:4

- Don't join the bandwagon of hate toward nonbelievers. Instead, seek the counsel of those who are trustworthy.

  He who walks with wise men will be wise,
  But the companion of fools will suffer harm.
  PROVERBS 13:20

Let Love Define You

I want to value and serve my closest friends and family as Jesus served His own disciples. I hope they will not just hear of doctrine, dos and don'ts, shoulds and shouldn'ts, and manners and chores. I hope they will feel the touch of Christ, the compassion of Christ, and the encouraging words of Christ through me. I hope they will learn to love Him because they have felt His love in the minutes of our lives together. But growing in love is a process of and takes a long time to ripen into maturity.

I hope I will also love those who choose to be harsh with me, even if they never change. When I do, I know I will find peace, because the more I make choices like Jesus did, the more I will sense His pleasure and understand His sacrifice in the midst of the many people who despised Him. Just as the Lord said, "I will never leave you or forsake you," so I will let my beloved ones know, "I will never leave you or forsake you. I will be praying for you, I will celebrate life with you (and cook for you, give you gift cards, call you, and pray for you when you are far away from me). You can tell me anything, and I will be your friend and companion as well as your leader and guide. I am here for you, I have your back, I love you, love you, love you. . . ."

Most of us who have been involved in ministry over the years have experienced divisive and broken relationships within the Christian community. Just because someone attends church, calls herself a Christian, and says she has a quiet time every day does not mean she will be a trustworthy friend. (And it doesn't necessarily mean I am a trustworthy friend. We all have blind spots.) But there are a few principles of wisdom I have learned over the years that are helping me navigate difficult relationships and that I will share in the "Own Your Part" section below.

Overcoming and learning to love is often one of the most difficult choices we make when we have been wounded, treated unjustly, or used by those who lack the same commitment to love. Yet when we give in to the unbiblical standards of others, we just diminish our souls and stunt our own growth.

Sacrificial love takes us on a journey to the deepest places of our souls. It requires a death to self, but in the end, it leads to a deeper, more mature appreciation of what it really cost Christ to redeem us. It is then that we will begin to share in the deep fellowship of God as a kindred spirit and truly begin to take on the image of Jesus.

✳

Own Your Part

Not long ago, I found myself very hurt in a relationship. Personality issues and a disagreement on our ideals had broken the trust between us. Having been in ministry for over forty years, I was not totally surprised, but any broken relationship hurts both parties. Yet by then I had learned that God is big enough to hold my cares, fears, and hurts and that when I try to carry things that destroy my heart's energy, it drains me too much.

Psalm 131:1-2 has become a pattern of commitment in my life:

O LORD, my heart is not proud, nor my eyes haughty;
Nor do I involve myself in great matters,
Or in things too difficult for me.
Surely I have composed and quieted my soul;
Like a weaned child rests against his mother,
My soul is like a weaned child within me.

So this time, I sought to be like a child before God—"This is too much for me to carry, and only You can make it right in the long run. I am like a baby in my need. I rest against You and leave You to solve this dilemma, which is out of my control."

When I hand over my pain to Christ, peace fills my heart, even though the hurt may resurface once in a while. I just acknowledge that my Jesus will hold this mystery for me in His capable hands and solve it in His time. Here are a few other ways I've learned to overcome negative responses to others:

1. "Guard your heart above all else, for it determines the course of your life" (Proverbs 4:23, NLT) was written by Solomon, supposedly the wisest man who ever lived! *Guard* means to watch over, protect, put borders around. If you are lonely, don't jump into relationships. Instead, trust God, seek to be friendly

and interested in others, but take your time in giving the depths of your heart to another—as you are opening your life to the possibility of foolishness or hurt.

2. "Behold, I send you out as sheep in the midst of wolves; so be shrewd as serpents and innocent as doves" (Matthew 10:16). Jesus Himself acknowledged that when we go into our world, we are being sent as sheep among wolves—even in the church at large. Everyone is at a different level of maturity. When I begin spending time with a new friend, I have learned to be aware of warning signs to avoid long-term hurt. If a woman is constantly critical of others; carries lots of drama; tells me secrets and then always says, "Don't tell anyone"; is fearful, gossips, or is not humble but defensive when corrected, I see these as cautions.

   We are to be humble and loving toward all people, but we need to develop discernment in relationships. Scripture says that "Jesus, on His part, was not entrusting Himself to them, for He knew all men" (John 2:24). Seek to understand the direction of the heart of the person to whom you are considering entrusting your heart.

3. Look for wise, mature, trustworthy people with whom you can be close friends. Don't trust your secrets, fears, deepest desires, and dreams to someone who has proved to be immature in the past. Seek out people who inspire you to love Jesus more, who are humble of heart and trustworthy in character, and who do not gossip or hide anything from others. As Proverbs 13:20 says, "The companion of fools will suffer harm."

4. Philippians 4:7 (NIV) instructs us in guarding the imaginations of our hearts: "The peace of God, which transcends all understanding, will guard your hearts and your minds in Christ Jesus."

When we find ourselves enmeshed in a hurtful relationship, it is tempting to obsess about the hurt and the unfairness of our situation. We may even engage in "he said, she said" sorts of conversations in our minds. Some of this is the process of figuring out issues and getting back to our center after we have been hurt. But, honestly, I have found that focusing on that which we cannot change and storing bitterness is neither productive nor healthy.

I have learned to write out in prayer the issues that repeat themselves in my brain—and then I write, "This is Your issue to resolve, God. Show me where I am wrong, and in the areas where I have been wronged, help me to forgive. Lord, this is Your burden to carry. It is taking too much brain space and time space in my life. I give it to You to care for and resolve, because it is too much for me."

After praying such a prayer, we can leave the matter in God's hands—we do not need to allow it to steal our joy or energy. In time, God will work out His will. It only destroys us when we're eaten up with unproductive thoughts; we only create further bitterness that steals from our prayer time and joy.

Praying with You

Dearest Father, God of unconditional love, we understand how much You hate division and strife, and yet You came to die for us so that even these relationship flaws would be covered. Teach us about Jesus in our difficult relationships. Help us to make loving, generous choices. Thank You that all of our faults in relationship issues have been paid for and covered. Help us to grow in love to please Your heart. We come in the name of Jesus, our own soul friend. Amen.

CHAPTER 12

HARVESTING A GODLY CHARACTER

Owning Your Integrity

All life demands struggle. Those who have everything given to them become lazy, selfish, and insensitive to the real values of life. The very striving and hard work that we so constantly try to avoid is the major building block in the person we are today. POPE PAUL VI

Sow with a view to righteousness,
Reap in accordance with kindness. HOSEA 10:12

"SALLY, HELP!"

My friend's early-morning phone call roused me from bed.

Hearing her words at such an early time made me think something was terribly wrong or important.

"What's up?" I whispered as I tried to clear my morning voice.

"Remember when we were talking last week and you told me that most of your accomplishments—starting your ministry, raising your children, keeping your home routines going, writing your books— have required a whole lot of hard work? I am just now getting it. You meant hard work, over and over and over again. I thought that would last for just a season, but it never seems to end."

Though my friend had just begun her day, she was already overwhelmed at all the tasks ahead of her. I actually love to get these early-morning "friend" calls. My precious, kindred spirits know I want to talk to them anytime—just as I'm always ready to talk with my very own children.

"I have had such ideals about how I was going to live my life as a wife, mother, and adult, because my own home was so broken and dysfunctional," she said. "But I didn't even know how hard it would be to do the work of life. I was never trained to work, to do chores, to be responsible. I was raised in front of the television and on fast food. Learning how to be a real adult is killing me!"

And so go many letters I receive. How I can identify with them. I am an idealist. I can think up scenarios of a civilized life, where children do not fuss or make messes, marriages are in perfect harmony, and somehow eating three meals a day leaves no messes! Creating an elegant philosophy of life on paper or in my mind is one thing, but living out such ideals requires a will to work, lots of sweat equity, and perseverance! Even then, it is never totally under control or in any way perfect. And generally speaking, life is so far short of the romantic scenes we envision.

Yet to live life well, to invest in what matters, to begin to meet the needs of our friends and family, and to stay strong through the different seasons always requires so much from us. It's what I call character—the internal attributes that determine a person's external integrity and work ethic. Character provides the foundation of spiritual and moral strength that rules life decisions, commitments, and faithfulness. Owning your character is essential to making wise decisions, to taking responsibility for your actions and behavior, and to living a faithful life through every season.

Unless we own the fact that the choices and actions we make in life will indeed have important consequences, we will make flippant, easy decisions that kill the potential of our becoming strong and fit leaders in our homes and communities.

We are surrounded by leaders and pastors who have compromised their lives and made immoral decisions. The "heroes" of our day have not accomplished great feats of courage or sacrificed their lives to serve others. Instead, we worship actors, sports figures, and media personalities, not because they are virtuous, but mostly because they are powerful, rich, or popular.

When a culture has no heroes to inspire, no models of integrity to capture people's imaginations, the level of dignity, decency, and nobility declines. No culture in history has ever risen to greatness when exercising moral corruption. As a matter of fact, such compromise of basic virtues always precedes the decline of a country's influence in the world.

> *Character provides the foundation of spiritual and moral strength that rules our decisions, commitments, and faithfulness.*

In the Garden

Becoming a prolific gardener has always been my wish but never my strength. As a small child, I entered one of our own purple irises in a garden show with the help of my mother. My arrangement took first place, and that experience began my lifelong love of flowers.

I was fooled into thinking gardening would be easy when we relocated to Colorado one spring. Myriad wildflowers swayed gracefully in the ballet of springtime breezes, charming me to my tiptoes as we moved into our home. Colorado mountain meadows quivered with lavender, columbines, blue flax, and fat purple lupines. I pictured the flowers as evidence of angels' hands that had invisibly woven a rainbow of colors by scattering and splashing millions of seeds in the crevices of rocks, the flat meadows, and the hillside shade.

Given the living patchwork all around me, I supposed having a beautiful garden would be easy. I felt like Laura Ingalls Wilder, ready to subdue my land. However, living at an altitude of 7,250 feet now for nearly fifteen years has taught me that gardening and producing flowers require the skill, insight, and patience of a master gardener—and lots of hard work. And I had zero experience, training, or skill. Our home is located on the side of a mountain, which means my soil is rocky. Most flowers do not grow in rock, but in soil.

Not only that, it also seemed we had garden pests hidden everywhere. One year we planted 250 bulbs that I had ordered from Holland. Anticipating coral tulips, yellow daffodils, and brown and purple irises, I planted with vigor and fertilized the beds at just the right time. As the snow fell, I just knew my wonderful bulbs were receiving extra moisture that would help them grow even taller.

One morning as the snows melted and the tufts of mountain grass began to push through the cold ground, I looked out the window and saw a small herd of deer munching on my sprouting bulbs. Like a crazy woman, I ran out the front door, berobed, barefoot, and bed-headed, screaming wildly and flailing my arms at the deer. I felt they were laughing at me as they slowly sauntered off.

Next came the cute little bunnies. Quietly they munched on the sprouting plants until I found them one day and shooed them away. Then came spring hail the size of golf balls. The result of all those uninvited pests? I had a total of two blooms that year.

I spent many years searching for garden shops that specialized in high altitude roses, wildflowers that required little sun, and blue flowering bushes that bloom in rocky ground. I also learned how to keep the deer and bunnies largely at bay, and how to properly cover my garden whenever the skies threaten hail. Now I finally have a relatively lovely garden a few months of the year.

Seeds of Promise

When we look at a tiny seed, we can't see what will bloom from that minute speck of nothingness—the color, the fruit, or the size of the plant. There is vast potential locked within that seed, and under the right circumstances—planted in good soil, watered, and covered in sunshine—a miracle will happen. The seed transforms into something more than itself—it produces a plant that blooms and brings beauty, life, and color—and this is a miracle. Something seems to emerge out of nothing.

Our own lives are seeds of promise, holding the potential for becoming so much more than we can visibly see at the beginning of life. And yet the seeds of our lives are sown in a fallen garden. They require special care and the skill of a Master Gardener to grow healthy and strong. Only then will they bear what they are capable of producing.

God has placed seed potential in each of our lives. We have the potential for blooming, so to speak, but we also require wise tending to grow and to thrive. Our potential can also be snuffed out. This world is full of hazards, dangerous outside influences, and pests that can wreak havoc and diminish our lives. Fortunately, God, as the Master Gardener, intentionally left us instructions on how to cultivate lives that can thrive, even in a world where the conditions are less than perfect.

> *God has placed seed potential in each of our lives. We have the potential for blooming, but we require wise tending to grow and to thrive.*

Wisdom: Developing a Strong Moral Character

As we grow in godly wisdom, we fuel our hearts, souls, and minds so that we can live righteously. Godly wisdom is a theme laced through all the books of the Bible. Other resources speak to its power as well. I particularly like one of the definitions of wisdom I found in the *Oxford Dictionary*: Wisdom is "the soundness of an action or decision with regard to the application of experience, knowledge, and good judgment."

The more you gain wisdom through your life experiences, the more you gather biblical truth and instruction, and the more you apply good judgment based on what you've learned, the more likely you are to live a thriving Christian life. To become a person of integrity and strong moral character requires wisdom, application of that wisdom, and lots of practice.

Whatever you practice, cherish, believe, habitually think, and speak every day is what you are becoming. Your life cannot be separated from your character. It is directly related to what you sow. It's no wonder that gardening terms are used often in Scripture.

The prophet Hosea, for instance, tells us to "sow with a view to righteousness, reap in accordance with kindness" (10:12).

The word *righteousness* means living by moral goodness and virtue and doing what is right. For Christians, Jesus is our standard of righteousness. Yet God also gave us Proverbs, a book that overflows with practical admonitions of wisdom for living righteously.

In Proverbs 4, a father hands down instruction in wisdom, reminding his sons that "the path of the righteous is like the light of dawn, that shines brighter and brighter until the full day" (verse 18).

Even as we see the first inklings of the sun beginning to bring a dim light into the darkness of night, gradually the light overwhelms the darkness, and the full horizon of a sunrise illuminates the early morning sky. So is the development of righteous character in our lives, which happens little by little, shining brighter and brighter as we mature in character.

We obey God's commands in order to build our lives on foundations that will stand and not fail us in the storms of life. We live with virtue so that others can look to us as beacons that will show them the love and redemption of God. Our virtue should help in our outreach and draw others to us, not send them away.

When God called us to be lights in a lost generation, His desire was that, through the virtue of our purity of life and behavior, we would become guides to those who long to move from darkness into light.

Even as my garden bloomed only when I cooperated with the nature of our environment, so we thrive when we obey the spiritual laws that God created. When we support the very design God built into His creation by celebrating right living, the universe supports our cause.

Becoming the best you can be requires that you own your integrity and live the most virtuous life possible. What practices create a morally strong and virtuous life?

Because we reflect the character of God, Christians should be the most trustworthy, hardworking, truth-telling, dependable, moral, patient, and grace-filled people. This is our heritage from God. Our integrity comes before our influence.

In Psalm 15:1-2, David speaks of those who dwell with God: "O LORD, who may abide in Your tent? Who may dwell on Your holy hill? *He who walks with integrity, and works righteousness, and speaks truth in his heart*" (italics added).

Basic wisdom principles guide us in wise living, yet they often seem hidden in a culture that considers morality relative to each individual, that sees all decisions about life as equal, and that promotes the idea that everyone should be free to decide what wisdom truly is according to their own feelings.

Choices Have Consequences

Whether the voices are bloggers, movie stars, newscasters, media experts, professors, or experts of any kind, we are barraged with messages encouraging us to live compromised lives and to follow the foolishness perpetuated in the world. Even in ministry, people often hear voices giving them permission to live the way they want without considering the consequences.

Even though the world tells us we can get away with compromising God's standards, the apostle Paul reminded us that God will not allow for our excuses. He said, "Do not be deceived, God is not mocked; for whatever a man sows, this he will also reap" (Galatians 6:7). Believing the world's lie carries grave consequences.

The author of Proverbs offers this caution: "Do not move the ancient boundary which your fathers have set" (22:28). The seed a farmer sows determines the produce he receives. No matter what the world may say, if a woman sows foolishness, her life will reap its terrible consequences.

When I drive, if I follow the instructions that bring order to traffic, I will be more likely to drive safely, with no bad consequences. If I speed, follow closely behind another car, run stop signs or stoplights, or drive recklessly in drenching rainstorms or on snow-covered freeways, I place myself and others in danger. I am also more likely to wreck my car. There are consequences to violating the laws of driving.

Similarly, the choices we make have consequences. Foolish decisions bring foolish results. God, in His mercy, desired to help us know how to live well, so He gave us instruction about how to lead the best life so that we could avoid the dangers and pitfalls strewn in this fallen world.

Interestingly, wisdom is personified as a woman throughout the book of Proverbs. Wisdom teaches, wisdom calls out to walk in the ways of God, and wisdom prepares her table so that others can come fellowship with her and listen to her wise ways. The magnificence of God's imprint on women is that they are made to be civilizers in their worlds. Their capacity to educate, inspire, teach, and counsel is God ordained and directly tied to the pursuit of wisdom: "The beginning of wisdom is: Acquire wisdom; and with all your acquiring, get understanding" (Proverbs 4:7).

When a woman acquires stores of wisdom and understanding, she is a source of strength, security, and common sense to others who want to live shrewdly. It is a glory and a praise to women when they choose to exercise this capacity.

Planting Seeds of Wisdom

The larger the variety of plants and flowers I cultivate in my garden, the more beauty and blooms I produce. Similarly, there are many different seeds of character, each reflecting a different aspect of the beautiful character God wants to reflect through our daily lives. Scripture establishes the basics of a virtuous character, and these basic seeds of character help us define our goals as we seek to grow in wisdom:

- Tell the truth.

  You must not testify falsely against your neighbor.
  EXODUS 20:16, NLT

- Work diligently—don't be lazy!

  Poor is he who works with a negligent hand,
  But the hand of the diligent makes rich.
  PROVERBS 10:4

- Do what you say you will do. Be reliable—the kind
  of person others can depend on to keep her word.

  Know therefore that the LORD your God, He is God,
  the faithful God, who keeps His covenant and His
  lovingkindness to a thousandth generation with those
  who love Him and keep His commandments.
  DEUTERONOMY 7:9

  He who walks in integrity walks securely,
  But he who perverts his ways will be found out.
  PROVERBS 10:9

- Serve others.

  [Jesus said,] "Even the Son of Man did not come to be
  served, but to serve, and to give His life a ransom for many."
  MARK 10:45

  You, my brothers, were called to be free. But do not use
  your freedom to indulge the sinful nature; rather, serve one
  another in love.   GALATIANS 5:13, NIV

- Give generously, without expecting anything in return.

  A generous person will be blessed,
  for he shares his food with the poor.   PROVERBS 22:9, HCSB

- Forgive those who have wronged you.

  If you forgive men when they sin against you, your heavenly
  Father will also forgive you.   MATTHEW 6:14, NIV

- Guard and control your tongue.

  Those who guard their lips preserve their lives,
      but those who speak rashly will come to ruin.
  PROVERBS 13:3, NIV

  A gentle answer turns away wrath,
  But a harsh word stirs up anger.
  PROVERBS 15:1

- Choose to be a peacemaker.

  If possible, so far as it depends on you, be at peace with
  all men.   ROMANS 12:18

- Endure hardship with a humble spirit, as it will train you to
  be a faithful warrior in the battle for righteousness and will
  lead people to Christ.

  Suffer hardship with me, as a good soldier of Christ Jesus.
  2 TIMOTHY 2:3

- Persevere under trial and wait patiently on God to help you.

  Blessed is a man who perseveres under trial; for once he has
  been approved, he will receive the crown of life which the
  Lord has promised to those who love Him.   JAMES 1:12

- Don't gossip!

> There are six things which the LORD hates,
> Yes, seven which are an abomination to Him:
> Haughty eyes, a lying tongue,
> And hands that shed innocent blood,
> A heart that devises wicked plans,
> Feet that run rapidly to evil,
> A false witness who utters lies,
> And one who spreads strife among brothers.
> PROVERBS 6:16-19

There are so many more areas of wisdom to follow. Yet the point is, if you ignore or violate the principles of wisdom, you will experience devastating consequences in your life. In short, you are to seek to reflect the character of Jesus every day in all of your behavior.

The Christian life is defined not merely by the tenets you hold or the spiritual philosophy you espouse but also by how you choose to live every moment. When you listen to the voices that give you permission to compromise the ideals God has written on your heart, you ultimately injure yourself. Living righteously requires a discipline of will. To live a life of integrity means making choices every day, all the time, to practice righteousness. What you practice, you become. Or in gardening terms, whatever you water will grow.

You must choose to discipline your mind and direct your thoughts to pursue faith, goodness, grace, love, and truth. You must choose as an act of worship to cherish and hold to the virtuous ideals that are a part of God's heart—loyalty, sacrifice, unconditional love, long-suffering, faithfulness, diligence—and to guard your heart from the vices that will destroy virtue—hate, anger, laziness, despair. When you sow seeds of righteousness every day, little by little, the seeds will bear fruit and your godly character will be formed.

Soul shaping is hard work. Often planting these seeds pushes against your own selfishness. Excellence requires that you cultivate and uphold your own inner standards in a world that constantly makes concessions.

Much of your soul character is developed in the invisible moments of life. Sometimes the small actions, or seeds, that God asks you to sow do not seem to promise anything:

> so small a task as cleaning up after someone who has left a
>   mess—without complaining
> so invisible the attitude as choosing to be a peacemaker rather
>   than stewing in anger
> so hidden the labor of love as getting out of bed one more
>   time to soothe a crying baby or staying up late to listen
>   to a heartbroken teen who has been rejected by peers
> so insignificant as graciously serving another meal to a
>   disgruntled, grumpy spouse
> so overlooked as living alone with no one to care for you and yet
>   choosing to believe in the goodness of an invisible God
> so unseen as the choice to overcome the temptation to control
>   your circumstances by releasing your expectations into God's
>   hands, trusting Him with the unknown

These are hidden moments where virtue is built, where seeds of righteousness are planted. Yet you are asked to believe in the potential and latent miracles inside of these small life seeds before you can see the fruit.

You are to sow with a view to righteousness—not completely seeing or knowing the vast potential of what is in your hands. But your task is to be faithful to sow, by faith, the seeds of promise given to you, to cast the seeds of promise into the soil of life, generously, diligently, faithfully.

And God's task is to do the miracle: to take all of the faith seeds, love seeds, integrity seeds, and faithfulness seeds that you planted when no one was looking and to grow them into works of great beauty. Soul building takes a lifetime, and it requires self-discipline and a heart that can imagine how goodness, innocence, and beauty can change a world. Yet soul work is the stage upon which the messages of your life will be told and heard. As Paul noted, "He who sows sparingly will also reap sparingly, and he who sows bountifully will also reap bountifully" (2 Corinthians 9:6).

Living a life of influence requires practicing a life of righteousness. Own your character, and you will grow stronger in almost every other sphere of life:

> spreading the good news in faithfulness to the gospel
> serving your housemates or children, and loving and helping
>   your spouse
> praying and believing when no answer is in sight

In time, in His hands, there will be such a bounty of beauty, such a life-giving harvest from the seeds planted in life, that you will finally see that He was creating the miracle right beside you—a harvest of righteousness and redemption beyond what you ever could have imagined. But the harvest comes only to those who plant, water, cultivate, and wait by faith, believing in the promise of what lies ahead.

❋

Own Your Part

When I first moved to Colorado, I was introduced to an older friend who immediately became a kindred spirit. She was someone with whom I could share dreams and struggles, laugh and travel with, learn from, and love unconditionally. I did not realize just how much I needed her until we invested regular time in each other's lives.

A master gardener teaches the less experienced how to cultivate with skill. A wise woman becomes wise by copying other, more experienced wise women. We were not meant to become wise in isolation but to partner with others who care about us and who can help us, over a long period of time, to live into our potential.

1. Ecclesiastes 4:9-10 says, "Two are better than one because they have a good return for their labor. For if either of them falls, the one will lift up his companion. But woe to the one who falls when there is not another to lift him up." Look for women in your life who might disciple you or those who might mentor you through their books. They can help instruct you how to live more wisely.

2. Take some time to develop a long-term plan for growing stronger in character. I list three attributes every six months or so that I want to work on in my life. For instance, gentleness, wisdom, and faith are the attributes I have been working on for the past few months. I have picked books to read to inspire me and made specific goals in each area. Choose gentle words and listen with your eyes to the people God brings into your life.

3. Hebrews 12:12-13 teaches us to work on the areas of our lives that need to be strengthened and healed: "Strengthen the hands that are weak and the knees that are feeble, and make straight paths for your feet, so that the limb which is lame may not be put out of joint, but rather be healed." It is God's will that we become strong, and so He admonishes us to work and stretch toward healing and growth when we confront difficult areas in our lives.

Praying with You

Dear God, let us see the potential for a beautiful harvest springing from our lives, if we will only believe in the seed potential in our lives today, this moment, which by faith will become a harvest of righteousness beyond measure throughout our lifetimes. Amen.

PART 5

Owning Your Life by Loving Well

Create a Lasting Legacy

CHAPTER 13

PURSUING LIFE'S MOST DEFINING COMMITMENT

Owning Your Choice to Love

The hunger for love is much more difficult to remove than the hunger for bread.
MOTHER TERESA

[Jesus] said to him, "'You shall love the LORD your God with all your heart, and with all your soul, and with all your mind.' This is the great and foremost commandment. The second is like it, 'You shall love your neighbor as yourself.' On these two commandments depend the whole Law and the Prophets."
MATTHEW 22:37-40

CHRISTMAS IS A MEMORABLE BUT DAUNTING SEASON FOR ME. This is the time when I celebrate with those dear to me, so I constantly but freely give of myself. Now that all four of my children live out of state, they return home with consummate expectations of Norman Rockwell proportions. They anticipate our yearly tea luncheon for our oldest and closest friends, as well as the evening open house where we make music and sing carols while enjoying favorite sweets, savories, and everything in between. Throughout this season, there are gifts to give, cards to send, and adult children asking me to make one of their beloved favorite dishes.

Preparing one more meal should not be that big of a deal, but I must admit that the constant cooking wears me down. I am so thankful for the secret places where I can buy some meals ahead of time that can be stored in my freezer.

Yet I have learned that love can sometimes be spelled E-A-T! When I ask my boys why they love coming home so much and why they feel so close to us, their mutual answer is something like, "It's at the feasts around the table where we share life, hearts, fun, and memories while eating great food. It's where we are all friends within the same community." So I bribe them with meals and then tell them to love Jesus!

In fact, many of our holiday traditions center on food. There is what we call our shepherd's meal—hot potato soup and crusty home-made herb bread with fruit, cheese, and nuts—on Christmas Eve and cinnamon rolls on Christmas morning while we look through our stockings. (Yes, even the adults all get stockings.) And did someone say New Year's eggs Benedict? (All these recipes I learned by myself over the years from studying cookbooks and experimenting!)

The past few holiday seasons have filled my soul with great memories, but they've also left me out of breath and panting from the noise, activity, and loud discussions when we gather together to catch up on life.

One day at the end of the holiday season a year or so ago, only my third-oldest child, Nathan, remained at home. My other children had already left town to go back to their jobs or school. Nathan, however, had gotten a cheaper flight that left the next day. I was deep into my list of to-dos and on a rampage to get life back together when he moseyed into the den and smiled sleepily.

"What's for breakfast?" he asked, testing to see if I was up for one more "Mama made" meal. Soon after whisking some eggs together, I handed him his plate of scrambled eggs and toast. Then I started to walk back to my pile of papers, which seemed to be calling my name, but changed direction midcourse and chose a chair near him—to soak in a few more moments with him, knowing they were rare.

Sipping his tea as a meal ender, Nathan looked over at me and gently said, "I am so glad to have a few minutes alone with you—just you and me. You'll miss me tomorrow, but those papers will still be here, Mama! Could we talk for a few minutes?"

It wasn't just my delicious eggs he wanted; Nathan wanted my ear and my focus. He wanted me to cherish this moment with him. Love, in this instance, was spelled T-I-M-E. Would I choose to put aside my responsibilities and turn all of my attention on him?

I have learned the hard way that a passive "uh-huh" spoken with no eye contact or heart engagement fools no one and eventually alienates our loved ones. And so I chose to return my wholehearted attention to the living room and linger with him.

As Nathan stretched his six-foot-three-inch frame over the frayed maroon recliner, his ankles hanging off the end, he barely spoke out loud. "Mama," he said, "I love Rachael so much; I just never knew what it would be like to be so in love! I just had to tell you how I really feel about her."

My son's big blueberry eyes tend to have heart-melting effects on my mama heart. I tucked away my busyness and drive to get organized for the moment, cherishing the memory of the friendship we shared. That became my focus. I knew the tasks would be screaming at me tomorrow, but then he would be gone.

"Mom, I never knew I could love someone this much." His innocent eyes shone as he beheld the mystery of the love he felt for his fiancée, who had also become precious to our family.

"I just can't imagine living life without her," Nathan added. "Rachael has become so dear to me."

This love had changed him. I realized it would cost him more than he could ever know, but for the moment, it was fueling his willingness to give his time, finances, and future to the one who held his heart. His young love provided the impetus to begin the journey of giving himself away.

"Just wanted to tell you," he said, smiling, "since you are my other best friend."

The Power and Choice of Love

Love is the magical, mysterious power that connects us deeply to others. Love binds our hearts, gives us a sense of belonging, inspires great acts of sacrifice and courage, and cultivates emotional healing. Love is demonstrated by acts of compassion, care, and comfort, and it holds the secret to extending the influence and reality of God to the world.

Loving another person is not logical, but it is a highly intelligent decision that promotes insight into life. Those who love have a number of things in common:

Lovers always want to share in the companionship of their beloved.

Lovers are captured by a constant flow of thoughts of their beloved.

Lovers enjoy just being with the one they love, as often as possible.

Lovers delight in making their beloved happy.

Lovers give up their own expectations to serve or please the other.

Lovers want to share their whole lives with the one they love— their thoughts, dreams, discouragements, feelings, every part of themselves.

Lovers change their priorities and live with greater energy and focus because of the value the beloved has in their heart.

The essence of God is to love and be loved. He is the One who crafted love and made us with a deep hunger and need to be cherished.

God is the author of all great love stories. We long to live a God-sized story, but all great stories begin with love.

There is a reason that all of life is a symphony to be played together in community. There is a reason we seek the security of a place to belong within the melodies and moods shared by loved ones.

When God considered how to ensure that pleasure would fill our hearts, He thought up friendship. Companionship is where we can relish the intimacy of being known and still loved; it's where dreams are heard, broken hearts are soothed, play is mutually enjoyed, and ideas are expressed.

We long for friendship, family closeness, and attachment. God designed us to feel the need to belong, and He created community and romance so that our desire for close connection can find fulfillment. Loving others is the oxygen that breathes satisfaction and happiness into our souls. This is why maintaining close relationships can be a battle in a fallen world: because they are essential to our well-being. Deep friendships are often so very hard to find because this is the fallen place. And yet intimacy with others is what our souls were made to experience.

Yet as our culture has come to prize efficiency, utilitarian values, competency, and materialism, we have become isolated and alone. We have drifted further from the very foundation of life that sustains us—the need and desire to be loved, accepted as we are, and validated for our own uniqueness. And so we have settled for sawdust in our souls.

Loving well is nonnegotiable if we are to live thriving, emotionally healthy lives. Babies fail to thrive without love. Many studies suggest that adults who are in loveless or lonely situations are much more prone to life-threatening illnesses. We cannot thrive in isolation.

Measure your life by how well you have loved.

If I could give you only one encouragement in this book, it would be to measure your life by how well you have loved. In the moment that you love well, you are the most like Jesus.

God is much more concerned with your love than with your service. If you truly love Him, then acts of service will naturally follow. However, you can do works of service without loving Him or anyone else. As the apostle Paul wrote in 1 Corinthians 13, such good deeds will only be like a noisy gong or clanging symbol.

Mature love—demonstrated by serving others through a heart of giving—is the only way we will ever truly come to understand and know God. But love truly is a choice, a commitment that demands your time, attention, grace, and humility. It's a choice that you often have to make in the inconvenient moments of life, or when the people in your life are irritating, frustrating, or immature. You must own your choice to allow love—both your own and Christ's love—to be extended to others through you.

Humility Enlarges Your Heart

When I was younger, I am sure I was a bit self-righteous and patted myself on the back for the ways I pursued my ideals and worked hard to live a strong Christian life. I have matured little by little over the years, but I am still sometimes shocked at the pettiness, lack of patience, or sudden anger that rises inside of me without warning!

This self-understanding, though, has made God's love toward me even more precious. The truth is, none of us deserve the love we receive. No matter how hard we try, we are selfish creatures wrapped up in concern about our own well-being.

Today I better understand Jesus' words about a prostitute who had failed much in life. He essentially said, "She who is forgiven much, loves much" (see Luke 7:47). The more I see the dark places of my own heart, the more humble I am as I think that He would honor me so by adopting me, pursuing me, and providing for me. How does He even put up with me? Why is He so patient with me when I am so likely to sin?

Love, I realize, is more fully given from a heart that has been humbled. Out of my gratefulness for God's love, I am able to have more compassion for those who fail, knowing that I have failed too. Because I long for patience from others, I am more able to give patience when needed. Since I have felt the sting of rejection from those who should have loved me but didn't, I am more devoted to giving my children and husband the love I longed for from my own family and friends through difficult seasons.

Love develops through a process of growth, practice, and exercise. To say "love is messy" is a cliché, but it is nonetheless true. Loving others is not a formula to be followed; it is unique for each relationship.

I find it interesting that when Jesus admonishes us to love others, He never asks us to love in ways that He has not already loved. Jesus was the model of love, and we see Him living it out in the stories of the New Testament.

Jesus loved the man who had leprosy and touched his scabby skin in order to heal him.
I loved by cleaning up and comforting my young babes after they'd thrown up.

Jesus loved by lifting an adulteress out of the sand and giving her the grace of a new life.
I had to love, forgiving others and extending the grace of Jesus' love to those who had terribly wronged me, when I felt like living in anger.

Jesus loved by stopping what He was doing to take children into His arms to bless them, listen to them, and value them, even though His disciples thought He was too busy.
I learned to love by giving up projects and a career outside the home to read one more storybook, correct one more attitude, and attend to the hearts of my four around-the-clock little ones.

Christ served, healed, pursued lost sheep, and dove into the messed-up lives of those He cherished. When Jesus asks us to love Him and love others, He has already modeled what that looks like through His life.
I learn to love by giving up my rights, my expectations, and my pride so I can give from a humble heart of generous love instead. That is what Jesus did for me.

Though I'm never perfect at loving and make many mistakes along the way, I realize that following the pathways of love has led me to the most deeply gratifying accomplishments of my life.

- Serving and building abiding relationships with my children have resulted in the best and deepest friendships I have ever experienced, now that they are all adults.

- Investing intentionally in my husband and learning to persevere in love with him through dark and difficult times have created a legacy of marriage that has lasted through all seasons and left a heritage to my children and generations to come.

- Teaching and sharing God's messages in ministry, as well as opening my home to literally hundreds and hundreds of people to whom I've served meals and welcomed as guests, have led to an influence all over the world that rose from serving, loving, writing, and giving—one hour, one day at a time.

All of these have consumed my world, my time, my energy, and my devotion. They have required all the years and the best of my life. Yet building these relationships has brought me more pleasure and a greater sense of accomplishment and validation than anything else in my life. The rewards were worth the sacrifices.

Love Profoundly Changes the World

Loving well is the best and most profound act of life. Learning to love helps shape us into the kind of people we long to be. It has led me to confess my bad attitudes, stretch to become more self-giving, and ask for forgiveness when I've failed. Seeking to love God with all of my heart and to love others as myself is an act of obedience that has built more of God's character into the deep places of my heart than any other practice.

Love done well is lived in the messy, demanding details of life and requires split-second choices to invest in its power. It often requires that we go against the ways of the world. It forces us to reach out to those who are different, to those who are offensive, and to those who are needy but can't give back. But when we follow God's ways, we understand better

Loving well is the best and most profound act of life.

that His will is good, acceptable, and perfect. When we obey Him, our own hearts become freer and more beautiful. It's as simple as that!

The grid through which you see your life will determine how well you love. If you truly believe that the way you love God and others will determine the success of your whole life, your life will reflect that priority. Your grid will tell you:

This is a moment to lay down your work and listen.

This is someone who needs your help.

This is a person who needs your time and who longs to be accepted.

This situation requires your service.

This is a young woman who needs affirmation through words that build up and fill in the holes of her heart.

Jesus said, "Whoever has my commands and keeps them is the one who loves me. The one who loves me will be loved by my Father, and I too will love them and show myself to them" (John 14:21, NIV).

You gain the eyesight to see God when you give your life to serve in love. The more you lay down your life, the deeper your gratitude at His willingness to pay the cost and lay down His life for you.

You don't love others because they deserve it. You love them because Jesus commanded it and because you love Him. You love out of an appreciation for how generously God has loved you.

If love has not become the grid through which you live your life, then your life cannot be filled with the love of God. It is His focus,

His priority, His value, His model, and His teaching. Loving others is required through all the demanding moments of life.

I've learned that many of the lessons in loving well are taught in the home, in marriage, and in parenting. The day after Nathan opened his heart to me, he returned to his life in Hollywood, where he has been seeking to be an influence for God. With his new love for Rachael, who is now his wife, his heart has been tenderized to the influence love has to change the world.

This e-mail came a month after he returned home from the last Christmas we shared:

Hey you,

I was just taking an easy morning preparing for work later and thinking about you. I just wanted to let you know that, in complete honesty, I can't say I've seen someone love out better, stronger, or more humbly or passionately than you.

I know that your passion and love for Jesus have and will continue to change the world and be the reason millions come to Jesus. I was so lucky to have had such an amazing example and picture of someone who is sold out for His Kingdom. Because you lived your life in such a beautiful pursuit of Him, it has enabled me to live fully the story God has for me to tell.

By your faithful example I love Jesus with all my heart and want to change the world, all because you made a choice to make everything you do come from your love of God.

I sure do love you today; just thought I'd let you know how blessed I feel to have had you in my life.

Love you, Mama—you're the best.

Nathan

Love is not always convenient, but when you choose it, the results are better than you can imagine. The years of loving my wonderful boy were filled with laughter, tears, fusses, messes, apologies, immaturity, and service; yet in the end, the process of staying with it built a tapestry of relationship that brings such deep smiles to my heart.

Love begins with a choice and a commitment; in the end, love is a legacy that will be remembered forever.

---- ✳ ----

Own Your Part

Late one evening after spending time with friends who'd returned from international ministry in a very difficult country, I was yawning repeatedly and longed to be in bed. Yet the Holy Spirit was tapping on my heart, telling me I needed to give a word of confidence to our weary friends. They had told many stories of the challenges, faith, and loneliness they had experienced overseas.

I grabbed a note from my drawer and quickly wrote, "Your model of giving to others is such an encouragement to our family. Though we know your labor is so very difficult in a country closed to the gospel, we also know that God is with you. The Lord of Hosts is your protector and your Father, and He will use you to change history in the lives of people who long to know Him. Our family loves you and cherishes the legacy you are leaving. Know that you will be in our prayers."

I left the note outside their door. A year later, I received an e-mail from my friend. "Sally, I keep your card in my Bible. When I am tempted to give up, I read it. Your note encourages me again and again that I am not alone. Thanks for taking the time to love me through your words."

I had no idea that the one simple note had been so cherished.

1. Peter, who had walked the dusty roads with Jesus and understood his own need for love and forgiveness, penned these words: "Since you have in obedience to the truth purified your souls for

a sincere love of the brethren, fervently love one another from the heart" (1 Peter 1:22). What does it mean to love fervently—from the heart? This seems to be a directive. Who is in need of your special love? How will you show it to them?

2. "Love your neighbor as yourself." This statement from Jesus is simple but has such profound meaning. How do you love yourself? What does this imply for all of those around you—do they need the same grace, sympathy, help, kindness, words of encouragement that you need? Write a card to two people who are your neighbors and who need to know love.

Praying with You

Lord, we know that Your heart is filled with love and motivates all the ways You have reached out to redeem and strengthen us. Please show us how to be more consistent in loving others. Give us the grace to extend Your love to those who need to feel Your touch through our actions. Amen.

CHAPTER 14

CULTIVATING A SENSE OF PLACE

Owning the Atmosphere of Your Home

To invite a person into your house is to take charge of his happiness for as long as he is under your roof. JEAN ANTHELME BRILLAT-SAVARIN

The wise woman builds her house,
But the foolish tears it down with her own hands. PROVERBS 14:1

JANUARY THROUGH MARCH is always an overwhelmingly demanding time for our family. Since 1998, we have hosted conferences at hotels for thousands of women across the United States during those months. My goal during the weeks when we aren't traveling is to keep our normal life as consistent as possible.

Some years ago, I hired a young woman to help manage the details of our lives during this season. She handled the mail and phone calls, and she did light housekeeping. When we were out of town, she cared for our beloved golden retriever and made sure there was food in the refrigerator when we returned home.

Because she was the age of my older children, she began to hang around our family when we were home. Every evening we would gather around the table at dinnertime. Not only did we eat together, we also shared the day's events and just talked and laughed together like friends. One evening when this young woman was over, I had thrown together our traditional snack meal—what I refer to as my "punt" meal when I do not have lots of time to prepare. We had homemade bread, cheese, fruit, popcorn, crackers, hummus, nuts, and a few other items I'd been able to find in our cupboard.

The seven of us lounged together for a long time. Weariness had caught up with us, and we reveled in the soft candlelight, instrumental music, and time to share in peaceful conversation.

Then suddenly the young woman stood up and nearly ran from the room. I caught her in the hallway, where she was quickly donning her coat. As she began to head toward our front door, I saw tears streaming down her face.

"Are you all right?" I asked. "Can I help? What is wrong?" Gently, I steered her into my small study and shut the door. As soon as we sat down together, she sobbed as she poured out a storm that had been building inside for many years.

"You all have a place to belong," she said. "You are a part of each other. Everything a person could want or need—food, friendship, spiritual encouragement, rest, comfort, and fun—is here. It is so familiar to you that you don't even recognize the structures in place to support your lives.

"My mom and dad each divorced several times, so I have moved from one place to another. We stayed alive, but we did not truly 'live.' I realized tonight that this—a home filled with acceptance and comfort—is what I have always longed for. I want a place to belong, a people to be a part of, but I never really thought they existed, except in storybooks. As we were sitting at the table, I suddenly felt deep sadness and regret for all I never had and realized that this is what I want."

Homeless Civilization

With the breakup of homes through divorce and families' frequent moves from city to city, many people are separated from close family members. In addition to that, all of us can easily isolate ourselves from real relationships with our foray into the world of Facebook and the Internet, endless working hours, and long commutes. As a result, our society has lost its understanding of the concept and true value of home.

I am not even speaking of the poor who do not have a place to live. I am speaking of people whose basic needs for housing, food, and clothing are met but who do not have a sanctuary designed to preserve all that is precious in life. Such people do have dwellings—apartments, houses, dorm rooms—but they do not dwell in places where life is preserved, protected, and cultivated so that the daily needs of their hearts and souls are met.

Whether you are single or married, young or old, painting the reality of God onto the walls of your home will be one of the great works of your life. People long for holy shelter: a safe place of comfort that values and preserves all that is good and offers solace from all the pain life's issues can bring.

Rivendell is the name of the "Last Homely House east of the Sea" in Middle-earth, the world in which *The Lord of the Rings* takes place. An Elven refuge, Rivendell was a sanctified dwelling that kept alive all that had been good, beautiful, artistic, and delightful but had been lost through generations of war and doom. "Merely to be there," we read, "was a cure for weariness, fear, and sadness."[5]

Painting the reality of God onto the walls of your home will be one of the great works of your life.

Perhaps this is an apt picture for us as we seek to preserve truth, relationship, beauty, and goodness in our homes so that whenever someone enters, people will be surrounded by the good, true, and beautiful. God was the original creator of home, and He crafted the Garden for Adam and Eve. He designed the first home with their needs, pleasure, and purpose in mind. In Genesis 2, we learn that God Himself planted the Garden, which was full of benevolent wildlife and beautiful trees that produced delicious fruit. A river ran through the

Garden, keeping the plants watered and no doubt providing refreshment to all who dwelled there. Most important, God took time to walk and talk with the man and woman, who felt no shame or need to hide from Him.

From Genesis we learn that we were created for a place—the Garden; with a heritage—to be the children of God; and with a purpose—to subdue the earth and bring God glory in the midst of our stories. Because of the Fall, people lost their place and became wanderers; they lost a sense of their relationship with God and began searching for their identities in the vacuum of empty cultural choices; and they lost their sense of purpose and started looking for meaning in wealth, power, and status.

For centuries, people had to bear the consequences of living apart from God's original design. Then many centuries later, God drew His enslaved people out of Egypt back toward a land of freedom and blessing like the one He had originally prepared. Providing them with an identity as the people of God, He called them Israel. Understanding their need for purpose, He ordained them to be a nation who would worship Him and reflect His truth and love, and to be a holy people set aside to depict what it looked like for a people to be in relationship with the living God.

> Moses went up to God, and the LORD called to him from
> the mountain and said, "This is what you are to say to the
> descendants of Jacob and what you are to tell the people
> of Israel: 'You yourselves have seen what I did to Egypt,
> and how I carried you on eagles' wings and brought you to
> myself. Now if you obey me fully and keep my covenant,
> then out of all nations you will be my treasured possession.
> Although the whole earth is mine, you will be for me
> a kingdom of priests and a holy nation.' These are the
> words you are to speak to the Israelites."
> EXODUS 19:3-6, NIV

God made their dwelling place to be a complete sanctuary where life could be lived to its fullest. That is why defining the ideals for your home is so important—it, too, can offer others a small picture of how God designed us to live in community with Him.

Defining Your Vision of Home

An architect who desires to build a distinguished edifice must first make the blueprint that documents the design and placement of the structure's foundations, boundaries, facades, and enclosures.

Similarly, in order to build a vibrant, rich, life-giving home, you must create a detailed plan. You cannot build what you have not imagined. The size of the home is not significant. Whether you live in a tiny city apartment, a mountain cabin, or a sprawling country estate, your home is defined by its interior life, not by its size.

Out of my own need and desire to build a legacy-giving home, God helped me cultivate ideas for what the heritage of our home, the true laboratory of life, could become. These are the thoughts I wrote down in my journal:

Home is the foundation upon which great civilizations are built. It is the sacred dwelling where souls are forged, humans have great value, children are cherished, and marriage is regarded as holy.

Home is the place where virtue is shaped: Minds are fed great ideas, truth and beauty, the finest of writing, and the clearest of thinking. The food of thoughtfulness and insight is intentionally disseminated and protected every day.

Home is the place where moral excellence is modeled, learned, practiced, upheld, and honored daily; where innocence is allowed to grow; where holiness is prized; and where cynicism is kept at bay.

Home is the place where faith is practiced, cherished, embraced, and reflected in the very breath of life throughout all the days lived in fellowship with those who abide there.

Home is the haven of inspiration, where the art of life is expressed and taught. Color is strewn into every corner; delectable food is tasted; fine art, books, and beauty are strategically placed throughout the scenery of its rooms and walls.

Home is the place where the whispers of God's love are heard regularly, the touch of His hands is given intentionally throughout the day, and the words of His encouragement and affirmation lay the foundation of loving relationships.

Home is the place where stories of heroism, sacrifice, love, and redemption are celebrated and embraced and heard, shaping the dreams of the souls who live there.

Home is a place of ministry and the giving of redeeming words, thoughts, actions, and love to all who come under its influence.

Home ties invisible strings from the hearts of the children who live there to a history forged together, to a heritage defined and celebrated, to a calling that is shared by those with the same last name.

Home is the "bedroom" of family, the safe place where all thoughts and dreams can be shared, the resting place that decides the destiny and definition of life for future generations.

Home is the place designed by God as the laboratory of righteousness and divine calling for each one whose life was fearfully and wonderfully made.

What a grand and auspicious work a woman is called to; how significant and far-reaching is the scope of her vision. When she understands the breadth of her calling, generations will have their faith ignited, and those who seek truth will find it within the walls of her home. She becomes the voice of God to the one who longs for wisdom and understanding; the comfort of His hand to the one who requires relief; the kindness of God to the one who longs to be seen; and the celebration of God to the one who seeks joy.

After refining these thoughts over the years, I implemented their practical application by designing rhythms of life, traditions and celebrations, decor for the rooms, a comforting atmosphere, and traditions to protect the ideals related to home. Some of the ways we've chosen to express them in our home include:

- bookshelves in every bedroom so that each family member can build a library with books that hold messages related to his or her own ideals
- a library/tea room with comfy chairs, a tea set, paintings, and candles and music, which provides a lovely getaway for heart-to-heart conversations
- a well-stocked kitchen where I make all kinds of fare from homemade recipes collected and crafted over years of testing and then shared nightly over a table of fellowship
- a basket of books and a chair in each bedroom to encourage reading and quiet time, during which God can speak to our hearts and minds
- musical instruments—from a piano to guitars to penny whistles—for practicing and producing music that creates a sense of worship and celebration
- clusters of chairs, grouped together to encourage close conversations; rockers on the front porch; settees and big chairs on the back deck

Each room is filled with "life treasure," often gleaned from garage sales or secondhand stores over many years.

You now know a few of the ways I've tried to live out my ideals of home. Yet all the habits, rhythms, and values stored in what encompasses the vision of "home" cannot be laid out in one chapter in a book. (Perhaps that will be the subject of my next book!) The point of this chapter is simply to inspire the vision for what a home can be.

In the end, however, it is not the actual details or rules of a house that give it meaning. Rather, the heart and attitudes behind the palpable moments shared within the home are what is most important.

Because I have had years to build my home's atmosphere, to create traditions that cherish relationship and family history, and to develop practical plans to keep it all running, my home has taken on more character and definition with each year. We all have a lifetime in which to build the legacy of home through differing seasons.

Attitude of Home

The reality of having at least six people eating, living, sleeping, playing, getting sick, and celebrating holidays together meant that my house was constantly in a state of disarray. That reality makes me think of this image from Scripture: "Where no oxen are, the manger is clean" (Proverbs 14:4).

As I look back now, I have to agree with all the sages before me: I wish I had not been so concerned with the messes and had instead set aside more time to take mental photographs of all the precious memories, moments, and stages.

A few years ago, we were visiting a family in a city where I was speaking. Everything in the home—I should say, estate—was perfect. We found a garden without weeds, a home in perfect order, and a meal with no mess because all the pots and pans had been washed and put away before our meal. Yet something about the environment seemed sterile and stiff to Clay, our children, and me. The children were quite rigid and formal. They seemed afraid to move out of an air of "reserved politeness." The atmosphere seemed barren and lackluster, and we felt somewhat uncomfortable—almost as if a mysterious aura of performance and judgment pervaded the rooms. As we ate dinner, the mom repeated three times, "I am so exhausted all the time."

As we drove away, we talked about the strange, almost palpable atmosphere of stress and strain we'd felt, even in the midst of perfect order. Everything appeared so right and yet felt so wrong.

There seemed to be form without art or life.

I am not condemning order or high ideals. I love both! I am guilty of holding the highest of ideals. But if the ambience in the home reflects performance and not heart, all will be lost. And frankly, we all have been in homes where we've felt a subtle pressure to perform by not saying the wrong thing and where peace, comfort, and love seem to be absent!

If we exist under a cloud of perfect performance, we will end up like Martha in Luke 10—stressed and strained by all of the work to be done. Yet if we accept that wherever people dwell, there will always be clutter rather than static moments of order, we will be freer to enjoy what is being built there.

Often, in this culture, we carry around images of house beautiful. The atmosphere of our homes, though, should reflect our views of God. If we consider Him pleased with us and generous in His Fatherhood because we are His beloved, then affection, humor, and happiness will be manifest in all the moments of living. But if our goal is to have a perfect environment, then anger and harshness will permeate our homes and dissatisfaction will whine through our conversations. Home will not be a place that invites but that discourages.

Too often, we carry a warped attitude about God in our hearts, as though He is cross, angry, and terminally disappointed in us for not being perfect. But God is not crossing His arms, looking scornfully down His nose at us and saying, "Well, I was going to encourage you today and tell you how much I love you. But I can't—look at that pile on your desk! I'm shocked at those mounds of laundry, and I am suspicious because you have been laughing too much today!"

Instead, He delights in opportunities to say,

"Woo-hoo! You invited a lonely person in for a bowl of soup
even though it made you miss that deadline."
"You sat with your child and watched Me paint a sunset!"
"You were patient with that spilled milk and broken vase when
your visitors were careless and created more work for you."
"Once again you listened to that weepy teen into the wee hours
of the morning even though you were exhausted!"
"You took the initiative to host the out-of-town missionaries
[or the foreign exchange student] even though your life is
already demanding."
"You are My precious one, and I love that you are doing your
best to attend to the needs of others and clean up the messes
that are made in the midst of all the activity."
"I love you; I am with you; I am proud of you because you
keep going!"

People often ask me why I emphasize beauty—art, candles, music, cups of tea, cinnamon rolls, great stories and books—as though these things are unnecessary and frivolous. I prioritize them because I want to bring the whole reality of God and His life into my home.

A home is a place of life, filled by a woman who exudes a contagious sparkle in the midst of messes and laughter in the midst of duty. Her song pervades the whole place. Music, feasts, art, and celebration flow out of a heart that has found joy in her God.

Home: A Place of Discipleship and Relationship

Many years ago, I began writing about the ideals of home because I longed for a place that would provide my family a sense of place. I wrote during the days when I had four children, ages twelve and under, along with a constant stream of company trekking through our revolving front door.

To build a home of ideals means a life of sacrifice. It means a lot of work, and it's never going to be over. These ideals don't come easily to anyone; they come through battle. It's an illusion to think that building a place of beauty ever happens naturally to anyone; it happens little by little . . . through hard work. . . . When we cultivate our souls, our kids will have something to draw from. The house with the life of God isn't a perfect house, it's a redeemed house! It's not a home without sin, or without messes or without spilled milk, but we redeem one more moment, in the joy of living with Him, and that moment becomes a memory, an unspoken message that lasts for life.[6]

Consequently, living out our ideals at home is not about reaching perfection, but about providing peace, hope, life, vision, and love to our families. Today, in the midst of all the messes, go ahead and smile, laugh, sing, and dance to the rhythms of God's song.

A home is a place of life, filled by a woman who exudes a contagious sparkle in the midst of messes and laughter in the midst of duty.

The making of committed followers of Christ occurs in relationship. Deep relationships are a result of investing time, expressing love, meeting needs, and patiently praying for those we are serving. Seeking to transform hearts to love and know Jesus more personally is the profound work of my home.

In my time spent studying Scripture, I observed Jesus interacting with His disciples for three years straight and hanging around with crowds that pushed, pulled, jostled, and shouted at Him. I read how He took children in His arms when others would have sent them away. All of these things give me a picture of what my life as a home-cultivator is all about.

Seasoning in the art of love requires time, experience, and humility. Discipleship is the work of a lifetime, and it comes . . . sometimes slowly . . . in fits and starts . . . two steps forward, one step back . . .

when we develop a long-range vision and believe God's promise that our work will not go unrewarded. Grace is the heart attitude that grants others the freedom to listen and learn so that as they grow, they master the skill of cultivating long-term relationships.

Grace moves me to extend all that I am for the benefit of those under my roof. It is the heart attitude that offers acceptance and forgiveness as Jesus did, or kindness when a soul is lost and troubled. A heart serving for the sake of Jesus will always have more energy to fill the cupboards of souls with the never-ending food of mercy, kindness, and compassion.

Grace encompasses:

- giving a cup of cold water to a thirsty visitor
- setting a bouquet of flowers on a winter windowsill
- speaking a kind, patient, timely word
- rescuing a four-year-old who drops his plate of food or spills another cup of milk
- writing a personal note of encouragement to a hormonal girl who wishes that someone understood her
- enduring a sleepless night to sit with someone who is broken and just needs to be held
- offering a back rub and chocolate chip cookies to an overwrought teenage son struggling with feelings of awkwardness
- saturating your kitchen with the sounds of instrumental music, light from a burning candle, and the aroma of a warm meal, all prepared for a grumpy husband who is worried about finances when he comes home from a hard day of work
- sending an "I am so thankful for you!" note to a weary coworker
- pouring a cup of hot tea and making time to listen to a heartbroken friend
- going on a mountain walk at sunset with someone who needs a break

Grace is the undeserved and unforeseen act of kindness and patience that totally transforms moments. It is the noble soul exercised toward the humble, broken, weary, and needy, without thought of returned favor.

Home is the stage where the play of your life is delivered. As you clarify your vision, accept your limitations, and cultivate grace, you are laying the foundations that will build influence and legacy.

Homes built this way are necessary if we are to continue passing down righteousness, hospitality, and grace from one generation to the next. If you long to increase your influence, then own your home life right where you are. Your quiet and consistent labor will result in a story spoken with gratitude long after it has been given in the service of the One who is creating an eternal home for us in heaven.

* * *

Own Your Part

Since our home has been filled for so many years with people who have needs, there are obviously times when I am weary and spent . . . and then comes one more day! A friend of mine sent me this note in December: "Our pennies are fewer than ever with a child in college and another one who needs a car soon, but I have a special Christmas gift for you. At your leisure, I want you to bring yourself and two other people to my home for a breakfast planned for your pleasure!"

I chose my daughters as the friends to bring since they were home for the holidays. When we arrived, homemade hollandaise sauce was bubbling on the stove, eggs Benedict was being prepared, and monkey bread and a large pot of coffee adorned the table. I felt as though I were at a queen's feast. To have someone take the time to serve me was about the most loving and wonderful gift I had been given in a long time.

I thought of Proverbs 24:3-4, which says,

> By wisdom a house is built,
> And by understanding it is established;
> And by knowledge the rooms are filled
> With all precious and pleasant riches.

1. What ideals do you want your home to reflect to those who enter? What are three ways in which you can build your home into more of a haven of rest, comfort, and beauty?

2. Proverbs 14:1 tells us that "the wise woman builds her house, but the foolish tears it down with her own hands." How will you build a legacy of faith and love through the rhythms of your home life? What factors do you see in your life that might "tear down" your home or the relationships or faith in your home? What do you need to do to gain control over that area? Television, phones, and computers can steal from personal time or lead to bad attitudes and anger. Be practical and honest as you consider what may be preventing you from bringing more of God's life into your home.

3. In order for you to be a conductor of beauty, goodness, and love in your home, you need to keep filling your heart so that it has the strength and endurance to keep giving. What are two ways in which you need to pull back from stress? What are two ways in which you can refuel (e.g., a time-out alone at a café for coffee and quiet to plan your week, or a morning a week to sleep in and catch up on rest—whatever means the most to you)? Plan these into your weekly schedule.

Praying with You

Precious Father, You have gone to such great lengths to build a world that is packed with the beauty and artistry of Your hands. Help us to take the time to enjoy what You have made. You are creating a place for us for all of eternity. Help us to follow in Your footsteps and become homebuilders right where we are so that those who come into our lives may also sense a place to belong and a haven where they might find Your love and provision. Thank You for caring not only for our needs but also for our desires. Amen.

CHAPTER 15

BUILDING A LEGACY OVER A LIFETIME

Owning Your Marriage

Happy is the man who finds a true friend, and far happier is he who finds that true friend in his wife.   FRANZ SCHUBERT

They are no longer two, but one flesh. Therefore what God has joined together, let no one separate.   MATTHEW 19:6, NIV

FOUR TALL WHITE ROCKING CHAIRS grace our front porch, inviting those inside to come out to celebrate a lovely summer morning. Those who sit here look out onto the rosebushes I planted, as well as stately aspens and mountains. An hour spent here, sipping coffee or tea in mugs while gently swaying back and forth, provides a perfect repose and place to share secrets and bare one's heart in moments of uninterrupted quiet.

That is exactly what I pictured when I first bought the chairs. As my son and I were loading them into the car—with much difficulty, I must say—he told me, "You don't need four rockers; two are plenty."

"Oh, no!" I responded. "Don't you know that wherever I place chairs where people can sit, a group always gathers to share conversation or tell a story? Each area needs to seat at least four, and when I have more money, six, so we can make lots of memories talking."

Making our house into a life-giving home has taken years of planning and lots of hard work, money, and intention. First, we sanded the old, dirty, worn wooden floors and restored them to their beautiful original color, which had been hidden as a result of people padding across them with muddy shoes for years. The sunshine had faded them too.

Next we redid and rearranged the kitchen. We pulled out and replaced the twenty-five-year-old kitchen cabinets. We also added a granite island and a new high counter and stools. We carefully chose paint, tile, and color accents to create a warm atmosphere. Our labor in the kitchen required vision and lots of sweat equity. I wanted a sanctuary that invited cooking, drinking, munching, and great feasting on exquisite food, all shared and enjoyed together. That dream provided the energy to see the task to completion.

We also focused on enhancing the atmosphere right outside our home. Nurturing rosebushes required great perseverance, as deer munched on them and the snow killed off certain varieties. Our efforts paid off. After studying the terrain for many years and buying bushes over and over again, we now see hundreds of blooms bursting open each summer. We planted numerous aspens, which were mere twigs at the time. Now, at thirty to forty feet tall, the trees shimmer throughout spring, summer, and winter, as though always holding a secret song inside and dancing to the music of life. Between our roses, trees, and mountain landscape, the view from those rocking chairs is breathtaking, with the vibrant reds, pinks, and corals combining with the dancing, whispering leaves to provide a peaceful setting. This work of love shaped the hours I planned and planted.

We wanted to create a shaded area for gatherings in the back of the house as well. To do so, we pulled the back deck apart. By putting up a roof and expanding the space by a foot and a half, what had been a smallish, crowded area was transformed into an outside den. Now groups of friends can feast while almost sitting among the pines. Women meeting for Bible study and family who gather when our children come home all find shade from sun and rain. It is another space where we can feast, laugh, cry, and share moments together.

Bringing beauty, order, atmosphere, and service under our roof was a strenuous and time-consuming labor of love. Slowly, after years of perseverance, the charm and elegance of our home came together in a kaleidoscope of color and patterns. This place, carefully crafted, now reflects my own soul's imagination of what our home could become.

Shaping a Life Heritage in Marriage

Early one evening, as purple clouds sailed slowly over the distant Rocky Mountains, Clay and I gently rocked in our front porch chairs together, enjoying the cool mountain air. As we nibbled on a snack dinner, we began reflecting on more than thirty years of marriage.

"Did you ever think so many years ago," I asked, "when we were so young and in love, that we would be here in Colorado with four children and a daughter-in-law, an international ministry, numerous books under our belt, a legacy of messages that I hope will live after us, and our marriage still intact? God has pretty much outdone Himself for two such normal people."

When I look over the landscape of many years of marriage, I see it as a beautiful work of life, a partnership worked out through the good times, the dark times, the celebrating times, and the sad times. I entered into it as a young woman, not understanding that it would take intention, tears, forgiveness, faith, perseverance, loyalty, and a servant's heart to make our marriage last. Isolation and heart separation colored some seasons for both of us, but we faithfully took one day at a time. As a result, I now know what loyal love looks like because it held us fast and shaped a great story in the eyes of our children, who held us accountable.

The same is true of our home. We invested so much time and grunt work, even though sometimes everything simply looked like messes and piles of junk. Yet it got better with each new addition, growing more beautiful as we followed our ideals to fashion a welcoming and nurturing home.

Truly, I did not imagine how far God would bring Clay and me in our lifetime together. Yet "till death do us part" was our forever commitment. That, and our pledge to serve God together, was the glue that kept us together and enabled us to build a legacy that we hope will last long after we are gone. One of the privileges of my life has been to learn how to be a partner to my husband as we seek to serve Christ, advance His Kingdom through our work together, and raise our children to be spiritually strong, vibrant adults.

In the same way that my "home building" required vision, a plan, and a lot of hard work, so our marriage needed a vision, a foundation, and a mutual commitment to do the hard work of building a great story together.

Marriage: A Mirror of Our Relationship with God

Marriage is a work of divine art and a masterpiece created over a lifetime. To become valuable, it must be worked at, fought for, cherished, and invested in. Only then will it become the legacy God intended it to be—a heritage of stories of faithfulness, humility, forgiveness, traditions, and prayers. A long marriage, one seasoned and stalwart through all the events of life, is indeed worth pure gold.

Marriage is a work of divine art and a masterpiece created over a lifetime.

Marriage serves as a model to our children, illustrating the reality of what it looks like when two imperfect people pursue love and peace. We live out, in front of their eyes, how to face difficulties with faith, how to persevere through trouble, how to develop a work ethic, and how to become responsible adults.

Our children now look at our loyalty and faithful commitment to each other as the standard that feeds their own ideals. Each child has come to me independently to thank us for staying with the hard work and giving them a secure home community to hold them.

Joy returned from college last summer after being a resident assistant (RA) to more than forty-five young women and commented, "So few of my college friends came from families where their parents are still married. I think an old marriage that has grown more beautiful through the years, like yours and Dad's, is worth pure gold."

I have so many precious friends who have lived through the heartbreak of divorce. This chapter is in no way meant to be a condemnation of those who have divorced. God is the One who heals, renews, and restores all of us in our brokenness.

Yet God established marriage as a holy, eternal union that speaks to the very heart of life purpose. With that in mind, we need to uphold the ideal of marriage as God intended it before the Fall. Marriage is a lifelong work, a long-term story that moves toward a good ending if it is invested in, cultivated, and nurtured, with God's Spirit holding all the pieces together.

In Malachi 2:16, God said, "I hate divorce." Even as God would never abandon us or leave us, so marriage was created to be a picture of His everlasting commitment and loyalty to us. Once He is committed, it is forever. And so the marriage of a man and woman is to reflect God's beautiful, never-ending loyalty to us.

Own your marriage—take responsibility for building your union into a story worth telling for generations to come—and you will have a tale of God's faithfulness to repeat to your children and grandchildren. You will give them hope, energy, and direction as they build a legacy of righteousness in their own families someday. You will also be modeling God's faithfulness to His own bride, the church.

That's something I did not understand when I was first married: Marriage is a mirror image of our relationship with God. We were not originally made to live alone, and so when we commit our lives to someone, we promise to walk together and to shoulder any issues through all seasons as life partners.

God created the marriage union to be a reflection of His relationship with us. In the same way that two become one flesh, so God intends that we become one with Him so that He can love us, teach us, encourage us, and live within us through His Spirit. We are to cherish our commitment to Him throughout all of eternity.

When we become Christians, we make a life commitment to God. We pledge to walk together, hand in hand, never to be separated and to share in all the issues of life. We commit to serve Him, choose to honor Him, and live by faith in Him our whole lives. Our oneness with Christ can never end. God perfectly models this relationship for us in Scripture, calling Himself the Bridegroom, and us, the church, His bride. And so marriage is to reflect the unity of our bond with Christ—always mysteriously connected to our husbands as one, never to be separated in life.

God is the ultimate lover. Marriage is meant as a picture of our Bridegroom, Jesus, and His never-ending, unconditional love. He initiates and pursues a relationship with us. He values us so much that He gave up His life for us. He promises never to leave or forsake us; He says that nothing can separate us from His love. He forgives us for all past, present, and future failures; and He is preparing an indescribably beautiful place where we will celebrate and enjoy life with Him for all eternity.

The Costs and Rewards of Commitment

God instituted marriage and family as the primary communities through which people would find companionship, comfort, celebration, protection, and stability. When marriages flourish, culture is stable and strong. Yet no marriage thrives unless two spouses are dedicated to cultivating emotional health, laying foundations of sacrifice, and defining the divine purposes for which this intimate companionship was created by God.

After being married for many years, I have learned that as a wife, I must always continue working at our marriage. Even after the honeymoon ends and children become a part of a family, husbands still need their wives' undistracted focus once in a while, including time to talk to a faithful listener. They need their wives' attention so they can share their fears, dreams, disappointments, joys, battles, and desires. For those reasons, there will never be a year when it is okay for me to become passive and settled. Whatever is watered will grow—and a marriage always needs to be a priority in order to keep growing.

Each year brings a different set of challenges, and sometimes, we just have to put one foot in front of the other and wait until we can have time together. For a period of years, I had three asthmatic children who also had chronic ear infections. For the seven years before she died, my mom was very ill, and I had to make multiple trips to her home two states away. During those years, it felt as if Clay and I were both coming and going.

There is no formula or rule about how to keep working on your marriage, but it will always need attention and commitment to grow. God has given each of us a unique personality and background so that we are quite free to exercise our commitments in different ways.

Women are the heroines of life in my book. Women rock. Our very inheritance—being made in the divine image of God—gives us power to influence in many arenas. When we embrace our innate heritage as civilizers, life artists, counselors, teachers, and musicians bringing song to life, our influence is glorious.

A woman partnering in marriage can become a true reflection of great soul imagination. She can envision and build a legacy of righteousness within her own marriage and family that will give life to generations to come. The capacity to create such a story is latent in any woman filled with God's Spirit; yet she must recognize, develop, and cherish that potential for it to become as healthy as possible.

One August day over three decades ago, Clay and I committed to remain together "till death do us part." There is no possible way I could have understood the ramifications of that pledge. I was so young, innocent, unprepared, and selfish—but I did not know it!

Life had not yet prepared me for seventeen moves; seven pregnancies and three miscarriages; four children who would take from my body, time, brain, and patience; fires, car wrecks, illnesses, the stresses of paying bills each month on a ministry salary, personality differences, church splits, hospitalizations and surgeries, family illnesses and deaths, criticism, confrontations, loss of friends; and so much more.

I also did not yet know that my husband and I are almost opposites in our personalities. We looked at life from different perspectives. Yet we had similar vision when it came to our spiritual ideals, our values, and the goals we had for our children. Those similarities have been a source of so much life and energy, enabling us to work out a spiritual partnership that became something of value.

In the early years, struggling through our differences was often my normal way of life. I allowed the refrains of recurring arguments, different perspectives, and personality clashes to chain me to repetitive conflict over and over again. Yet gradually, as I recognized my own selfishness and immaturity, I began to stretch in my understanding, growing one baby step at a time. I knew that Clay and I had committed to each other before God and made vows to do whatever was necessary to build a strong marriage.

Vows, in God's eyes, constitute a serious covenant to uphold a promise. Clay and I felt accountable for upholding our vows, which we knew were taken seriously before the throne of heaven, and so we kept moving forward during the seemingly impossible times. We both knew that our marriage would be forever, no quitting allowed.

We invested over and over again as we strained toward mature love. That meant humbling ourselves so we could forgive and learn to speak words that blessed instead of words that wounded. Slowly I learned how to be a graceful kiss on my husband's life instead of a source of hostility. My love for him and my love for God stretched me to become more giving, more understanding, more joyful—one day at a time.

I began to realize that for most people marriage is hard—really hard—at times. But the glory of a great woman isn't that her marriage is easy and naturally romantic, but that she rolls up her sleeves and determines to build her marriage into a legacy of authentic substance and to weave the elegance of love into the moments, traditions, and fiber of each day, each year. When I yield to God's will in any area of life—including marriage—and am willing to wait, I will see that His will truly is good and acceptable and perfect.

As I look back over the years, I can also see that my husband was a steady presence for changing diapers, cleaning up after ill children, and staying up at night with our ear-infected children so that I could catch some sleep. He wrote a song for each of our children and rocked them to sleep with that song when they were toddlers. He paid bills and took out the garbage every Tuesday before the trucks came. He packed our boxes before every move. He organized life as I invested in loving relationships. He sought to help train our very unique children as I cooked and planned the traditions and celebrations. As a result, our lives were woven together through the years, creating a deeply fulfilling history that became more than either of us could have accomplished alone. But it all started with our vows—to cherish, honor, love, and stay faithful—and our commitment to keep them.

All marriages have seasons of darkness, because they involve two selfish, immature people with different personalities. But Clay and I grew to understand that our marriage would be the work of our lifetimes. Accountability and commitment kept us faithful and moving forward. Now our marriage is a badge of honor, an attainment of maturity.

Romance vs. Reality

Romance and attraction are usually the forces that bring a couple together. When dating, men and women often carry fantasized ideals and worldly, secular, media-driven values. They have not yet faced the obstacles and realities of commitment.

No matter what their ideals before they wed, the real work and glory cannot even begin until a couple marries and moves into the subsequent stages of life. It's similar to wrestlers entering the arena to compete in a match. Their strength and ability are not tested until they are allowed to compete.

Romance eventually runs into realism after the wedding ceremony. Most of us enter into a marriage with selfish desires. In our hearts, we expect our spouses to fill our needs, to love us well, and to make us feel valued. A lot of the initial attraction that leads to marriage comes from hormones at work. As those calm down, we must build on that foundation with mature love, self-sacrifice, and mutual respect. That process can actually lead to the two becoming one—if they see marriage not as an impossible difficulty but as the great work of life that is completed little by little, decade by decade.

To use another sports analogy, people can't learn to swim by reading a manual. They learn to swim once they jump into the water. So when a couple dives into life with a desire to learn and develop skills as lovers and partners in life, marriage has a place to grow. They can become one in heart, mind, spirit, and values over a lifetime.

Yet most people enter marriage without a true biblical vision for what God has in mind. Without a proper vision for the partnership of serving God together, building their children into a godly generation, and serving the Kingdom of God as a family, there is no glue or core of strength that will keep two separate individuals together.

Without a proper vision for the partnership of serving God together, there is no glue that will keep two separate individuals together.

When marriage is seen as a panacea for fulfillment in life—when sex is expected to be ecstatic and perfect, when love is expected to always be romantic and fulfill all our ideals, when we expect our partners to fill all the empty spaces in life—we have the wrong expectations of what a marriage is made to do. Marriages that begin that way get off to weak and ill-fated starts.

Upon returning home from the honeymoon, the couple who could, before the wedding, see each other often and yet have a break from each other to enjoy time alone, now have a constant companion, 24/7. That adjustment is a test to anyone's selfishness!

Then different expectations and ways of prioritizing must be worked out, as couples navigate work schedules, hobbies, life habits and preferences, and demands at home. Chores must be shared and divided; food must be bought and bills paid. Money issues—the way finances are made, saved, or spent—become a focal point all too soon, and for most young couples, there is never enough to go around.

These new stressors are often compounded by the fact that most couples live in a small space with nary a place to escape. The list of pressures also includes such problems as illness, broken-down appliances, car wrecks, insurance paperwork—and did someone whisper "children"?

The reason I write about some of the difficulties of marriage—including those Clay and I have faced—is to help young couples understand that they are not alone in their struggles to adjust to all the challenges that marriage brings. Struggles and guilt for feeling "unloving" can make a woman feel isolated.

Yet marriage is one of God's tools: He uses it to help shape us more into the image of Christ. For me, it was the platform upon which He began to teach me the meaning of servant leadership and self-sacrifice.

Owning a marriage by taking personal responsibility for its health is one of the most basic ways we worship God. Marriage is designed as a way to help us grow in selflessness, sacrifice, humility, and creativity. It is also the foundation from which we may craft a legacy of life for future generations. And marriage is the place where these important life values would be learned, because God's plan was good and crafted to befit us as humans. Divorce short-circuits personal growth.

Faithfulness: Your Ministry to God

I recall some very stressful months during one season of our marriage. Three of our four children were teenagers when we learned that one of them had a possible brain tumor, which led to lots of doctors' appointments and tests. I had a book deadline looming, Clay had a ruptured disc, and my mom was immobilized after breaking her hip. All of these demands required more from me than I ever thought possible.

Running at such a pace to keep all of these balls in the air left me gasping for breath and longing for attention and support. One evening I sat in my bedroom alone and cried about how unfair my life was and how alone I felt in my marriage. My needs seemed heaped upon piles of expectations that I wanted my husband to meet, even though he was living through immeasurable back pain and the stress of keeping our ministry afloat because I had no margin right then to help him.

Crying from the depths of my heart, I told God that I didn't know if I could keep going. I expressed my loneliness and feelings of desperation. In the quietness of my heart, I felt God speak to me: *Sally, what if the most important task I asked you to do for My glory was to love Clay well—to serve generously in your relationship with him, to choose loyalty, to practice being unselfish? Even if no one else knew, would you do that for Me? Because this place of being unconditionally committed to him for My sake—regardless of his actions toward you—is what I want from you as your spiritual service of worship.*

Our circumstances did not change, but my perspective began to change. I could always choose to worship God by being faithful, respectful, and loving to Clay, even if my feelings were not always 100 percent in agreement—I was to learn the real meaning of love by practicing it in my marriage. I also understood that living with faithfulness, loyalty, and sacrifice was the service that God wanted from me above all else.

It was the hidden service of my heart, which no one else would see, that gave me reason to begin investing wholeheartedly in my marriage. Who I was when no one was looking was a reflection of my true integrity.

I would do for God what I was not, in my selfish flesh, willing to do for Clay. In other words, I could love Clay, not because I felt he always deserved it, but because God had asked me to. And as I look back, Clay was doing the same thing for me, loving me through the hard times and serving me through some of the weary seasons of life.

Working together, sticking it out during the hard times, and learning to serve even when we felt too exhausted to give any more led to one of our best and most satisfying victories. The sacrifice, courage, and conquering in battle become the glory of the warrior who wins the day.

Marriage is a long-term trophy, a treasure with hidden jewels that must be mined throughout the seasons of life. My pleasure at learning the invaluable meaning of sacrificial love is what has drawn me closest to Jesus. Understanding how much it cost Him to love me, when I was not even looking to Him, was the divine lesson of my marriage.

When Feelings and Commitment Conflict

Most women feel hurt, isolated, unappreciated, frustrated, and angry many times in marriage. Know that this is a part of the journey.

Forging two such different lives is like sanding the scum off of old floors. It takes a lot of rubbing to make a smooth surface, and so it takes lots of polishing to make relationships smooth. And yet in the end, the beauty and shine are worth all of the effort—they are more glorious than could be imagined.

As women, we often place very high and unrealistic expectations on our husbands. We get false ideas about romance from movies, media, and television. A woman frequently comes to marriage hoping that a young, immature husband will give her the kind of love she never had in her childhood—hoping marriage will fill the emotional holes in her life. Often, we expect our husbands to be Prince Charmings every day, as well as being husbands, fathers, friends, and hard workers. I wanted Clay to be the "leader of the pack," but I realized that there were times that, if I did not initiate a time away or a date night, it would not happen. He so appreciated when I planned dates and intentional time. It took some weight off his shoulders.

Some years of marriage are downright demanding and depleting between work commitments, bad attitudes, sleepless nights, bills, moves, exhaustion . . . you know the routine. Learning to bear these burdens makes us become more adult.

I made a few personal commitments over the years that helped me through some of the stinging moments of my own marriage. Now I offer them to you:

1. Don't allow bitterness to fester. It will only hurt you and steal your happiness.

2. Reset your expectations so you don't live in a perpetual state of feeling hurt. This is particularly important if your spouse is less mature than you or never changes. Scripture tells us, "If possible, so far as it depends on you, be at peace with all men" (Romans 12:18). What can you do to maintain peace in your life?

3. Create spaces in your life and home that give you a sense of worth and happiness. Choose to practice contentment within your limitations. The happier you are, the less you will react negatively to your spouse.

4. Remember that your children want you and your spouse to love each other. Learn not to talk badly about your spouse to your children. That accountability can draw you to maturity, and giving your children the gift of a content mom is priceless.

Look for other women with whom you can connect as well. So many women are isolated—with no friends as neighbors, no family close by, no kindred spirits. As a result, their personal needs build and build. When an exhausted husband walks in the door from work, his wife may be tempted to expect him to meet the needs that God intended a community of family and other women to fulfill. We really do need the fellowship and compassion that comes from sharing life with other women in the same situation. Be willing to reach out and make time for friendship with like-minded women.

The Hard but Sacred Work of Marriage

The work of marriage—forging a holistic family; a strong, vibrant atmosphere of love; a place where righteousness is formed and upheld; a holding place for beauty, celebrations, traditions, comfort, and commitment—is sacred to God.

The beautifying of my home took many years and lots of time and money, but it resulted in an amazing, life-giving sanctuary. Likewise, marriage takes years to build and beautify, but when we intentionally honor and craft it, it produces a life legacy that will give hope, security, and instruction to generations to come.

Understanding that it truly is not good for man (or woman!) to be alone and that we were made to have accountability and community is one of the gifts of a long-term marriage. Sharing our burdens, memories, heartbreaks, and victories is a priceless treasure that comes only from faithfully journeying together as two become one.

The wise woman must accept this request from God: Will you be faithful for Me? Will you serve and love and give to your partner because you told Me you would serve Me your whole life and live in obedience to Me?

We cannot separate our righteousness as Christians from the way we value and honor our marriages and our husbands. God desires our faithfulness, and marriage is the place He intended it to be lived out.

God's vision for marriage held us fast during great times of testing. Since we knew that marriage was good, by faith we treated it as though it had great value. We saw in Genesis 1 that before the Fall, God had created marriage and the blessing of children as the perfect way through which life would be organized. As a result, we strove to reach the biblical ideal of making our home the place of spiritual work and a divine affirmation that God's ways are good.

It is amazing that Clay stayed with me. In my immaturity and with my selfish perspective on life, I created so much stress because I lacked insight into his personality, desired getting my own way, and had unchecked regard for my own opinion.

Marriage is not just about sex and hormones and romance, though these are of great value. More important, marriage is about two coming together into a partnership and accomplishing more for the Kingdom of God together than they could ever do alone.

> The LORD God said, "It is not good for the man to be alone;
> I will make him a helper suitable for him."   GENESIS 2:18

God fashioned the human beings He had created for companionship and community. And so He designed men and women to be uniquely suited as partners in the challenges of life. How beautiful that He found a way to ensure we would not have to face all the challenges of life alone, but that we could share in the responsibilities and joys with a beloved best friend and companion. Two people with mutual goals, dreams, and purpose can build a message and legacy of life together. "Greater love has no one than this, that one lay down his life for his friends" (John 15:13).

We lay down our lives, not once for all, but in the midst of each petty argument, each time we are confronted with a weakness in our husband, and each time we feel let down.

Our feelings of anger, impatience, neglect, and lack of appreciation all feel so valid in the moment of being hurt. Yet none of us will ever be able to live perfectly. We will all keep failing and creating conflict, even if we try hard not to.

Lay down your frustrations! Don't allow anger to grow or judgment to fester. It ends up hurting you, stealing your pleasure.

God invested in our relationship with Him by relentlessly loving, pursuing, carrying, forgiving, and providing. And remember that when we love well, we are most like Him.

※

Own Your Part

Clay and I spent a couple of days of our honeymoon in Santa Fe, New Mexico. While there, we happened upon beautiful wildflowers that were pressed between two pieces of glass and then framed. We bought this artwork as a visual representation of Jesus' words in Luke 12:27: "Consider the lilies, how they grow: they neither toil nor spin; but I tell you, not even Solomon in all his glory clothed himself like one of these."

We recognized in this humble gift a reminder that God would have to clothe our marriage, give us beauty, and make us strong. He was the mysterious third partner in our relationship who could make our commitment stronger.

1. What are the biggest challenges in your marriage? What attitude do you have about those difficulties? How can you seek to grow and mature in handling these stresses as a service of worship to the Lord?

2. Name three things you are grateful about in your relationship with your husband as it relates to your marriage and family. Write a card (or an e-mail!) to him, telling him several ways that you appreciate him.

3. What one area can you work on during the next six months that will add more peace and grace to your relationship with your husband? What do you think he wants you to understand about his personality?

Praying with You

Father, we are beginning to understand that our marriages are representations of our oneness with You. Our marriages are pictures to the world of what unconditional love and commitment look like.

Please give us Your strength, grace, and wisdom so that we can grow in mature love and commitment. And bring us peace, we pray, in Jesus' name. Amen.

CHAPTER 16

SHAPING GENERATIONS
TO COME

Owning Your Motherhood

The most important gift you can give your child is to help them begin a walk of faith with the God of the universe. From the moment your children arrive in your home, you are teaching them how to see the world, what to consider important, what to seek, what to love. As a mother, you have the opportunity to form your home and family life in such a way that God's reality comes alive to your children each day. SALLY CLARKSON, *10 GIFTS OF WISDOM*

The man called his wife's name Eve, because she was the mother of all the living. GENESIS 3:20

FURROWED EYEBROWS have always signaled to me that my youngest child, Joy, is troubled or carrying a mysterious burden in her heart. I've learned that I have to mine her depths to unearth whatever has put her eyebrows in such a knot of consternation.

Not long ago, I whisked her away to spend time with me while I was in California. With three children living in that state, I am always looking for an opportunity to speak or work there so that I can be with them.

As Joy drove up in her car, I could see her anxious brow through the window. At eighteen, she was already a resident assistant for more than forty-five students in her dorm and had just finished an intensive two-week interim course worth six credit hours. She'd also been busy practicing with the debate team for an upcoming tournament.

Having entered college at seventeen, Joy had been shouldering lots of stress, responsibility, and pressure for nearly two years. I knew she would need to unwind and begin to let go of the tension she didn't even know she was carrying, since all these life issues had piled on her shoulders gradually, one at a time.

We began the evening by taking a walk along the beach and then eating dinner together at one of our favorite restaurants. That set the stage for her to begin opening her heart to me. Hosting conferences has its perks because I always have hotel points that allow me to stay for free when I travel, so my next plan was to whisk her to the hotel where we had stayed many times while hosting our Mom Heart conferences in California. The familiar trappings of the hotel spoke comfort to our exhausted bodies.

Late that night, sparkling lights from cars on the highway and the surrounding buildings danced and flashed on the curtainless windows outside our seventeenth-floor hotel room, as candles provided the only other illumination inside the room. Joy was curled up, exhausted, bedecked in her nightgown, with the bottoms of her feet dark from the sandy beach we had just walked.

Grabbing a warm, soapy cloth, I gently began to wash her small, feminine feet. A tiny speaker sat on the desk, emitting the sounds of acoustic strings weaving an atmosphere of peace and filling the silence with soothing comfort.

Next I squeezed citrus lotion in circles and began to massage her toes and the bottoms of her feet while I quietly talked to her about how happy my heart was to share in these precious moments together.

"Mama, I have always, always loved ending my days with your blessing and love. It makes my heart peaceful," Joy whispered as she snuggled and curled more deeply into the soft comforter atop the bed. My mama heart filled with joy, and I knew we would now unearth the reason for the furrowed eyebrows.

"What is troubling you, sweetie?" I asked. "I can see it in those telltale eyebrows."

Joy sighed. "Living with and caring for so many young women

in my dorm, I get bogged down with their huge emotional baggage. Mama, you wouldn't believe how lost, scarred, fearful, and insecure many of these girls are by the time they're eighteen.

"I am deeply surprised and disappointed at how many of the girls tell me they have never felt loved or accepted. So many of them are searching for affirmation. They say they have never had their parents' attention; many lack basic integrity, social awareness, and communication skills. There are so many holes and scars in their lives at so young an age. Sometimes all their needs overwhelm me.

"Finally," she added, "I am beginning to understand firsthand just how important a role parents play in the lives of their children. When they haven't had attention and love from parents, these girls look for love in all the wrong places. They lack basic character training, like going to classes, finishing homework, and saying no to boys who want to impose on them. Why would parents have children and then neglect to pass on love, care, and heart training?"

Quite a little sermon, but the thoughts had been building inside Joy for months. As she released them, her eyebrows relaxed. Monologues and ideals seemed to have been bubbling over from Joy from the moment she came out of the womb. And now as a debater in college arenas, she thought in "speeches."

Own Your Motherhood

My own childhood had been pretty devoid of babies. As the youngest with two older brothers, I rarely played with dolls or even thought about being a mom. Just like Joy, I was driven from birth, and so as a young adult, I pursued a career and enjoyed speaking and teaching as well as developing messages and books. Frankly, I never thought about motherhood. It wasn't that I didn't value it, I just never ever thought about it.

Since I had never changed a diaper and had babysat only twice in my young adult life, children were foreign to my life experience. Then at thirty-one, I prepared to hold my first baby in my arms. Having been a working woman for ten years, I was used to speaking to large groups, traveling all over the world, finding validation in my work, and having weekends to myself. I anticipated that motherhood would be just one role I would play among my others. Truly, I was not prepared for the job.

Sarah, my first child, emerged after twenty-two hours of hard labor. As soon as she was placed in my arms, I was overcome with the miracle of her. I hadn't expected the deep connection I felt to this living, breathing human being who had grown inside of me and emerged as a tiny little bundle of sweetness who would wrap her being around my heart.

During the first few weeks of her life, of course, I was overwhelmed by her care. As I endured sleepless nights, I was upset by her crying, clueless about whether or not I was "doing it right." Yet in the following months, I was captivated by her smiles, which I knew were especially for me, and by the way her tiny hand began patting my chest. I wondered why no one had ever told me how amazing it would be to enter this divine role.

As I held her in my arms, rocking her to sleep late one evening, I sensed God Himself speaking to me.

Sally, I designed little Sarah as a masterpiece with her very own dark blue eyes, walnut brown hair, a personality you will discover bit by bit, and a destiny to fulfill. She is a treasure to Me. Would you take her into your life as My gift to you? Would you raise her for Me—to show her My reality, to give her an understanding of My ways—My love, My holiness, My creativity, My compassion? Would you prepare her for the role I have designed for her to take in the world as she becomes a beacon to her generation about My Kingdom ways? Sally, will you raise this child for Me, as one of the best Kingdom works I will ever ask of you?

Truly, I began to understand that God entrusts these little ones made in His image into our arms so that we can whisper the secrets of His Kingdom into their ears. Then they will learn to love Him and serve Him forever.

It was a defining moment of my life, and God's Spirit moved me to begin studying Scripture. I wanted to see what He thought about children and better understand the mysterious connection between mother and child.

I didn't have an agenda or something to prove. I was not anti-feminism, but pro–God's ways. I had a simple desire to try to follow what Scripture said. I wanted to please God with all of my heart and to seek first His Kingdom by following the biblical design for family that is central to His heart.

Mothers, I came to believe, were God's finest idea for how such a righteous legacy would be passed on in each generation. They were designed by Him to influence the hearts of children within the sanctuary of their own homes and to help shape them into the next generation of godly leaders. Mothers have the capacity to inspire messages of truth and hope, to model love and servant leadership, to build mental and academic strength by overseeing the education of their children, to lead in faith, and to build a haven of all that is good, true, and beautiful.

God intended for righteousness to be shared from one generation to the next by parents cooperating with Him. Parents are the ones who effectively pass on God's Kingdom messages and values and the mandate of loyal allegiance to Him. Jesus Himself was born into a family where a mom and dad were given the responsibility of teaching Him about God. The key to building healthy, godly souls is growing them to maturity in a home where the life of Christ is lived, breathed, and taught.

Satan would love to obscure such an important calling. No wonder our world has lost the imagination for just how important the role of motherhood is to the health of future generations.

As I look upon the landscape of our culture, I think that what is more desperately needed than anything else is adults who love God with all of their hearts, who practice righteousness, who have a heart to reach others, and who stand strong against the moral battles of this day. Yet a child does not grow into such a godly adult by accident.

Now after twenty-nine years of mothering, I am sure that God was whispering the secrets of His will into my ears and impressing eternal spiritual truths deep within my heart all along. His desire and His plan were excellent. From my experience, I know that biblical motherhood is a most profound and meaningful role when lived by God's design.

My children are the best "books" I have ever written and have become my message to the world. What I mean by this is that I know I could not write about having integrity if I were not living it in front of them. I could not speak of the Kingdom of God if I were not trying to be like Jesus in my home. Actually, God used my role as a mother to shape me more into His image. My children were His form of accountability and assured that I had living, breathing reasons to grow in character—daily! I knew my children's eyes were on me when I told them to work hard and be responsible. They had to see me model the same virtues.

A child does not grow into a godly adult by accident.

All Mamas Feel Inadequate

I stayed at home much of the time with my children. Although I traveled and spoke for our ministry, I gave up many opportunities so that I could be at home with my kids. Balancing both was my puzzle to solve. I realize that everyone's circumstances are varied and different, but owning the stewardship of my role as a mother was always one of my priorities.

But as a young mom deciding to make motherhood my focus, I faced so much loneliness and isolation. I made it through many dark and devastatingly difficult seasons of motherhood because I saw the heart of Christ and knew He cared.

When I consider the situation of young moms today, I feel compassion and a sense that they are desperate for direction, input, and wisdom. Many long for a brief break from all their responsibilities—a night of sleep or a couple of hours away from home. Yet these mamas don't know where to find this help.

They also have many questions: Should a mom work or stay home? How should she discipline? Should she be a grace-based parent or a traditional disciplinarian? Does a mouthy teenager need discipline or love? Should the family homeschool or send their children to private school or public school?

I rarely meet a mom who doesn't love and cherish her children. Yet so many feel lost in a sea of contemporary philosophies. Often, they live with pain from their own broken memories of childhood sadness. Others are under intense financial pressure, especially in the current economy. As a result, many have to work just to feed their families. Then there are the many sweet single moms who bear so much pressure alone.

Many of these women have never heard of the biblical call to motherhood. They may come from broken families that didn't model how to love children. They may not feel they have permission from their culture to choose to take time to raise their children. Many moms have just never considered or been taught the truth about their role in children's lives.

I can relate to their confusion and concern. So often I felt inadequate as a young mom, as though I were ruining my children. I always loved them, but many times I did not like them. When pushed to my limits, I would occasionally yell at them and then wonder why God had entrusted me with them. At times they pushed every button I had and drained every ounce of energy.

Yet embracing this role to raise my children out of my love for Jesus has shaped me more than any other work I've done. And now my children are my best friends. Even though they know me, they still love me, and we have so much fun sharing life together. The reality is, though, if children are neglected either by circumstances or by lack of vision or training, it will have a long-term effect on their lives and send them into adulthood without foundations of faith, security, training, and confidence in the ways of God.

Following are some secrets of motherhood I wish I had known earlier in my life:

- *Unconditional love is the foundation of healthy parent-child relationships.* It becomes the grace that fuels the development of strong, healthy hearts in your children. You can express your love by intentionally affirming them with your words, playing together, serving them, and honoring them as real people. You also demonstrate your love when you validate their unique personalities, give affection, and model the gracious love of God in your relationship with them. They can believe in the love of God because of what they experience in your home.

- *Time spent together is what communicates love to your children.* You can't influence them or expect them to adopt your values without making this commitment. Nor can you hope to be the one who will influence their faith, values, memories, and emotional health. They will love the people whom they spend the most time with, who respond to them most often. No gadget, toy, or experience can buy a child's love and allegiance if the mama does not give her child personal focus.

- *You are the mother your children need.* Be yourself. When you like who God made you to be, you give your children the invaluable gift of a happy mom.

- *Don't make your children an idol.* They were not placed on earth to fulfill your needs and desires. If you hover over them too closely or seek to control every circumstance, they will never develop their own character muscle.

- *There is no formula or exact way to ensure you are doing it right.* Every home and family culture has its own personality. Our family has been shaped by our unique tastes, ideas, favorite traditions, books, stories, ideals, and life adventures. It is our commonly held family culture that creates belonging and a sense of "This is who the Clarksons [or the Browns, Smiths, Lees, etc.] are!"

- *All children should learn Scripture and Bible stories.* God's Word provides them with His vocabulary, which He will use to speak to them for the rest of their lives.

  By training them in the foundations of Scripture, you will give them confidence to live by His truth when they go into the world. (Clay and I wrote and used the book *Our 24 Family Ways* to put this vocabulary in the minds of our children.)

  > **Every home and family culture has its own personality.**

- *All children resist training.* When you seek to shape your children's characters and train them to become responsible, you push against their selfishness. If they put up a fight when you correct them, it is not because you are doing something wrong.

- *Remember that God has access to their little brains.* He will give you strength, wisdom, grace, endurance, and an understanding of how to live well with them through all seasons. God cares about your children; He will partner with you to complete the task, using your instruction and the words you speak to them during devotions to communicate to their hearts.

- *All mamas feel guilty for what they have not done completely or well.* Remember, "Love covers a multitude of sins" (1 Peter 4:8). God is faithful and always involved, whatever the circumstances of your children's lives. Never, never give up praying for them.

- *It is never too late to reach out to your children to say, "I'm sorry. Will you forgive me?"* Or to say, "I forgive you and will be here if you ever need me." Jesus is the One who told the Prodigal Son story. The father in that passage is the model to us of what it means to always be watching for a prodigal child's return home. This father welcomes his son with open arms and celebrates their reunion.

Don't Do Motherhood Alone!

We live in a "go it alone" culture. That's partly from our society's philosophy and partly because we don't know how to find community. We have learned to live in isolation without even knowing that we are violating our basic inborn need for friends.

Solomon, the wisest man who ever lived, wrote, "Two are better than one because they have a good return for their labor. . . . A cord of three strands is not quickly torn apart" (Ecclesiastes 4:9, 12).

God did not create us to live life alone. As a way to keep myself from going under, I created moms' groups in each place we moved, all seventeen times. Sometimes I would just find a few moms and meet with them once or twice a month at a café or coffee shop. Other times, I invited women into my home once a month. We would study a book on mothering together, but often we just ended up talking, eating snacks, giggling, commiserating, and praying. These casual gatherings provided me with an outlet with like-minded mamas and helped keep me sane. These groups also gave our family people with whom to do life.

Be a friend; make a friend. Stay committed when possible. Live in community. There will never be a perfect match to your desires and needs, but when I committed to finding other moms, I almost always grew to love those who were quite different from me. I also learned to give myself to others who were lonely, as I had been.

Each group was as it was made to be. Now I have my own little community. My own team. My own squirrelly inner circle.

If you are an older mom reading this, remember what it was like to be in the trenches of motherhood. Then reach out to mamas in your church, neighborhood, or other arena. The most powerful ministry you ever pursue may be just giving a mama a break. Consider it a cup of cold water for Jesus.

The Power of Servant Motherhood

I have written six books about motherhood out of a conviction that it is a profoundly important role that shapes our culture today. So it is impossible to cover all the issues in one short chapter. Yet it was watching Jesus and observing His life that taught me the priorities that would most shape my motherhood.

Whenever I read about Jesus' last meal with His disciples before being condemned to die, I am drawn to the way He expressed His love for them:

> Before the Feast of the Passover, Jesus knowing that His
> hour had come that He would depart out of this world to
> the Father, having loved His own who were in the world,
> He loved them to the end. . . . Jesus, knowing that the
> Father had given all things into His hands, and that He had
> come forth from God and was going back to God, got up
> from supper, and laid aside His garments; and taking a
> towel, He girded Himself. Then He poured water into the
> basin, and began to wash the disciples' feet and to wipe
> them with the towel with which He was girded.
>
> JOHN 13:1, 3-5

Jesus knew He was calling His disciples to serve and to be rejected and persecuted. He was asking them to lay down their lives. No doubt His own heart was heavy knowing that one of these men would betray Him, turning Him in to those who wanted Him crucified. So before breaking bread and pouring wine, what did Jesus do?

He washed 120 toes.

The God who threw the universe in place stooped to wash the dirty, sandy, smelly toes of His disciples. What an example for us as moms! Clearly, He understands the constant chores and mundane work that fills my days.

He also shows me how to reach the hearts of my children. As Jesus prepared to send out His disciples to share God's message of redemptive love, He didn't bark orders or threaten them; instead, He drew their hearts to His by loving and serving them. Their memories of that night must have been powerful. Certainly the act of washing their feet distinguished Jesus from the other religious leaders of His day. Though He called them to a standard of holiness, He freely showed His grace and forgiveness to them as He tenderly washed and dried their feet.

I want to reach out to my children in the same way. As important as it is to teach them about God and His Word, I must first spend time with them, loving and serving them—even on the days when I'm tired or have other important items on my to-do list. Only when their empty hearts have been filled with my love will they be prepared to listen to what I have to say. Only then will my words about God and His love for them make sense.

Owning your role as a mother will shape not only your child but also future generations to come. Your labor of love has far-reaching consequences. And as you build another's soul, you will find that you are building your own soul as well. The excellence you invest in others will always grow in your own heart.

✳

Own Your Part

Our son Joel is a musician whose homes have been in Boston; Hollywood; Cambridge, England; Nashville; and Tijuana, Mexico. Yet the older he gets, the more he looks for opportunities to come home. One evening after dinner, we chatted while watching the sun set behind the mountains.

"You know, Mom, the longer I live, the more I understand that a child, no matter how adult, always loves having a mom to come home to! Your cooking, your voice in my life, your acceptance and understanding of my personality, and the comfort of our home all call me back to who I am amidst the busy, demanding world where I live."

Moms never outlive the importance of their roles in their children's lives. Even now, in my sixties, I long to have my own mom caring for me and comforting me in the stresses of life, even though it has been many, many years since I had my mama's attention.

1. Paul compares himself to a gentle, loving, nursing mother when he speaks of his leadership and influence in the lives of the people he worked with in Thessalonica: "We were gentle among you, like a nursing mother taking care of her own children" (1 Thessalonians 2:7, ESV). How is the gentle nurture of a nursing mother a way to reach the hearts of your own children? How do you need to change some of your attitudes?

2. If Jesus told you that the service He most wanted from you was to raise your children and teach them all about God and His Kingdom, what would you need to do to take this role more seriously? Write down two specific things you can do to cultivate a more meaningful spiritual impact on your children—or in the lives of children you know.

3. Proverbs 31:26 says, "She opens her mouth in wisdom, and the teaching of kindness is on her tongue." The word *kindness* in this verse has also been translated as *lovingkindness*—referring to the lovingkindness of God. Write down three ways you can more purposefully teach your children of God's attributes and His lovingkindness toward them.

Praying with You

Father, You have shown us how to parent our own children by giving up Your Son in order to parent and redeem us. Help us to learn more about becoming servant leaders so that we can willingly lay down our own lives to serve our children. Amen.

CHAPTER 17

LIVING INTENTIONALLY TO LEAVE A LEGACY OF FAITH

Owning the Influence Your Life Can Make

If you read history you will find that the Christians who did most for the present world were just those who thought most of the next. . . . It is since Christians have largely ceased to think of the other world that they have become so ineffective in this. C. S. LEWIS, *MERE CHRISTIANITY*

I have fought the good fight, I have finished the course, I have kept the faith; in the future there is laid up for me the crown of righteousness, which the Lord, the righteous Judge, will award to me on that day; and not only to me, but also to all who have loved His appearing. 2 TIMOTHY 4:7-8

"SALLY, I think all that talk about laying down your life for the Kingdom is kind of extreme. Don't you think some personalities are just more prone to pay attention to that part of the gospel and others focus on other aspects of Scripture?"

I have heard comments like this one several times. Let me explain why I think they are shortsighted. I have now lived through six decades and have seen many people end their lives with regrets. People who routinely made excuses—who lived in indifference to the voice of God, or who were controlled by fear, busyness, complacency, selfishness, or laziness—often feel remorse when they approach the last decades of their lives. Somehow they never moved forward to do something to own the stewardship of their lives. These are some common rationalizations:

> "We don't all have to be that serious about our Christian lives. Pastors or missionaries are called to be more serious than the average believer."

"God called certain people to lead, and I am an introvert."

"God wants me to be happy. I make decisions based on my own well-being."

"People need to learn to help themselves."

"When I get married, when we save enough money, when the kids are out of diapers, when my circumstances are different, when I have more time, then I will consider how to make more intentional decisions about how to invest my life purposefully."

Tomorrow will never come. Today is the day we have been given to take responsibility for our lives. Jesus calls us to revolutionary principles—to love, to forgive, to give to the poor, to live for eternity rather than to build our own kingdom on this earth, to be humble, to give up our rights. All of His ways call us to a new world order with values that are the exact opposite of those this world lives by. Clearly, while He walked on earth, Jesus was focused on God's Kingdom. He talked about the Kingdom more than sixty times in Scripture.

Seek first His Kingdom.   MATTHEW 6:33

My kingdom is not of this world.   JOHN 18:36

Your Kingdom come. Your will be done.   MATTHEW 6:10

Jesus did not create His Kingdom and His calling for particular personalities. He called all of us to take His words to heart, and He asked all of us to "drop our fishing nets," so to speak. But only a few have ears to hear (see Matthew 11:15). Jesus will rule forever. His authority will continue throughout the ages.

When we come to Him, we come under His authority and begin to grow into the ways of His Kingdom and submit to His rule. Serving King Jesus and living under His rule are present as well as future realities. Because the Kingdom was such a part of His message when He walked on the earth, responding to Him, following Him, and seeking to spread His Kingdom's influence are responsibilities, not just for those with a certain disposition, but for all those who are His.

A House of Mourning Brings Fresh Perspective

The flowers gently swayed in the light breeze as we walked up the gentle slope toward the gravesite. We had gathered that day with family members, some of whom we had not even met, and with a handful of my husband's friends who had aged just as we had.

As we walked together, we smiled, hugged, and admired all the kids who were present and had "grown up so much." Rain had been predicted, but it seems God was smiling that day because the clouds brought cool comfort but not a drop of rain. As Providence would have it, just as I was to finish this book, my ninety-two-year-old mother-in-law passed away. As a result, I had to take a break in my writing to spend a week saying good-bye to my sweet mother-in-law and, along with my husband and his family, making her funeral arrangements. Ecclesiastes 7:2 tells us that "It is better to go to a house of mourning than to go to a house of feasting, because that is the end of every man, and the living takes it to heart."

Serving King Jesus and living under His rule are present as well as future realities.

In many ways, Solomon was right, because each of us must contemplate the fact that one day our lives will end, and others will gather around to tell stories about how they remember us and how we influenced their lives. A funeral is a great time to reflect on life.

As we gathered at my mother-in-law's funeral, I was once again faced, in a very real way, with an opportunity to consider legacy.

It seems I have been to more funerals in the past few years than ever before in my life. People gather to try to say nice things about the ones who died, to remember stories, to honor their lives. A funeral should also be a great place to receive inspiration. Rarely, though, have I been to a service where I left feeling more inspired to leave a Kingdom legacy because I could see the fingerprints of God all over that person's story.

The apostle Paul, on the other hand, told a remarkable story with his life, so that even after his death, it continues to motivate us to live with as vibrant a faith as possible. You may recall that Paul, a Pharisee, was one of the earliest persecutors of the first Christians. Yet after his conversion on the road to Damascus, his life turned around 180 degrees. The rest of his life was filled with hardships: imprisonment, shipwrecks, illnesses, and stonings. He wrote nearly half of the books in the New Testament without a laptop or even a typewriter. Yet at his death, he left behind church leaders, thousands of converts, and strong churches.

That legacy infuses these words with uncommon power:

I have fought the good fight, I have finished the course,
I have kept the faith; in the future there is laid up for me the
crown of righteousness, which the Lord, the righteous Judge,
will award to me on that day; and not only to me, but also
to all who have loved His appearing.   2 TIMOTHY 4:7-8

As I stood before my mother-in-law's casket, I found myself wondering, *Will "my people" want to live a better life when they review my life story? Will the ending of my life be a celebration of the reality of heaven and the coming of our King in His glory? Will my story call others to live fully engaged, faithful lives for God? Will my words inspire?* I can only hope so. Often, we do not think much about our own funerals because we are too busy living.

Perhaps that is what we all do—live and live and live until we suddenly find ourselves needing to account for how we invested our years.

And so this week, in between many cups of coffee and writing like a crazy girl, I have been jotting down some things I want my friends and family to hear when I leave to see Jesus face-to-face:

My sweet, precious husband, children, and friends,

How I have loved being your wife, mama, and friend. We have been so close that I know you will miss me a lot. And I will take all of you in my heart! But haven't we had fun sharing life together? So many precious memories and so much love! We are so very blessed to have found unconditional love and to have celebrated our crazy selves through all our life adventures. I am forever richer because of knowing and loving you.

I will leave a few reminders behind for you, as that is what mamas always do! So I ask for your patience, please, just one more time.

Live in Jesus. Walk your road with Him, dance to His music, cry with Him, learn from Him, be with Him, tell others about Him. Every day, every year that I knew Him, He got better and better because I knew Him more surely for who He really is. Jesus satisfies, His ways bring peace, and His love brings healing. So just keep Jesus always near, and you will be fine in every situation. Never allow any circumstances to overshadow His reality. He is true, and He will always be with you—every day, every season. I am standing with Him and getting so excited for you to join me here.

Celebrate life, every day, as often as you can. He has painted sunrises to remind you that He is there at the beginning of the day and stars to dazzle you with His beauty at night. When your burdens seem heavy, look up. He has your back and your front. (And if I can, I will be cheering you on until we see each other once again face-to-face. There will be such a celebration!)

Don't waste time in guilt for never being good enough. He is good enough, and your nearness to Him makes you good too.

Love as generously as possible. Give grace to most everyone you meet, as you may not know their whole story or what made them that way. And you know that bitterness kills the mind and soul. Don't take on the anger or guilt of others; just wait patiently for darkness to pass. There will be light at the end of each night.

Never allow your circumstances to overshadow His reality.

Remember that if there is any way for me to smile at you from heaven, I will be smiling. When you remember me, think of me praying for you, believing in you, and thanking God for you, because the story of our lives of faith together will be told forever throughout eternity, and I hope my life and love for you will bring you hope in the years to come.

Carry on the Clarkson legacy. Pass on righteousness in your lifetime. Show others the love and grace of our Jesus, and then when their hearts are open to you, tell them about how they may know Him. Be sure to teach your children about Him every day and to live with integrity in front of them, because you are the first Bible they will read. We pass on His messages and righteousness from one generation to another. So be sure they know what it is they are called to do—keep it going!

Whether you create music, write books, cook a meal, plant a flower, or develop a website, do it for God's glory. He has gifted you amazingly. So out of thankfulness, use all that you have for His glory.

Like Paul, I have fought a good fight and finished the course God set out for me. What a relief and privilege to have been able to walk hand in hand with God every day and to have been a part of His Kingdom work in my lifetime. Oh, the miracles of seeing Him provide through all the years.

As you know, dark times and tests will come. But they are only temporary. He left us His peace, and He reminded His

*disciples and us that in this world we will have tribulation.
Then He reminded us to take courage. Take courage, my precious
ones, and hold fast, as this trial will pass soon enough, and then
you will have a story to tell.*

*Think of the party and feasting and rousing talks we will
have again soon when we see one another in heaven. It will not
be so very long.*

*Love you forever and ever and ever. Peace be with each of
you. Now the Lord and I are near and in your heart.*

So what about you? What kind of legacy do you want to leave?
What life messages are worth living and dying for? You have a God-
sized story to tell, a destiny to live into! Yet you must choose to take
a step of faith toward Him.

Now is the time; today is the day. Own your life.

Heaven will tell your story throughout eternity. May you live one
worth telling. May you leave a legacy of vibrant faith and a pathway
for others that is lavished with generous love and the kiss of God's
favor each step along the way.

---------------------------------- ✳ ----------------------------------

Own Your Part

My hope is that as you have read my story, you have thought about
your own life and the kind of legacy you will leave. There are so
many areas to grow strong in—faith, love, living in the power of
God's Spirit, marriage, parenting, friendship—and so much more
that I did not cover in this book. Remember that God has created
you with such spiritual potential to live within your personality,
your dreams, your life, just as they are, and to leave a legacy of love,
faith, and spiritual influence.

What decisions is He asking you to make? Whom shall you love?
How will you forgive? How will you serve? In what ways will you

make His light, comfort, truth, and beauty come alive in your life? I invite you to consider your answers as you reflect on the questions and recommendations below.

1. Think about the legacy you are leaving behind—even now, as well as after your life on earth is over. Are you content with what you imagine it will be? Can you identify any areas of your life that you would like to build into in order to leave a more godly heritage?

2. Practice writing your own good-bye letter to family and friends. Doing so can help shed light on the reality of the story you are writing.

3. Think of ways you can help those you care about start owning their lives as well. Perhaps you can share with them the insights you've gained and the strategies you're formulating. Remember that "two are better than one because they have a good return for their labor" (Ecclesiastes 4:9). As you share your journeys, you will be more fully inspired to take steps that will leave a life-giving legacy for others.

Praying with You

Heavenly Father, I know how much You love each precious person who has read this book. You have designed each of us with such tender care, and You know all of our circumstances. I also know You have so much love, wisdom, insight, and strength to give us as You reveal the purposes for our lives. I pray that we will fall more deeply in love with You and will give our lives to follow Your paths for us. May we discover the profound blessing of walking each day of our lives hand in hand with You, the living God. Bless us as we seek You, and favor us with Your grace, strength, and joy each step of the way. We come to You in the precious name of Jesus, with hearts filled with gratefulness. Amen.

ACKNOWLEDGMENTS

My life stories have been abundantly blessed by countless loving, generous, spiritually vibrant people who have invested in me more than I could measure. I am especially grateful for the friends who have been by my side in life and ministry, through dark times and celebrations. There are too many to name, but you know who you are.

My four children and Clay are included in this list of precious friends. I thank you for your love, generous spirits, patience, and constant service to all of our ministry dreams over the years. I could not have lived well without you. Together, our team has changed the world. I pray God's favor and grace for each of you and am humbled by your amazing commitment to Him daily! I love you all dearly.

NOTES

1. *A Little Princess*, directed by Alfonso Cuarón (1995; Burbank, CA: Warner Home Video), DVD. The film was adapted from Frances Hodgson Burnett's classic children's book of the same title.

2. See 2 Corinthians 6:17.

3. Richard Foster, *Life with God: Reading the Bible for Spiritual Transformation* (New York: HarperCollins, 2008), 135.

4. See, for example, Richard Schiffman, "Why People Who Pray Are Healthier Than Those Who Don't," *Huffington Post*, January 18, 2012, http://www.huffingtonpost.com/richard-schiffman/why-people-who -pray-are-healthier_b_1197313.html (accessed July 25, 2014).

5. J. R. R. Tolkien, *The Fellowship of the Ring* (New York: Houghton Mifflin, 1954), 219.

6. Sally Clarkson, *The Mission of Motherhood* (Colorado Springs: Waterbrook, 2003).

ABOUT THE AUTHOR

SALLY CLARKSON cofounded and has served as the women's ministry director of Whole Heart Ministries with her husband, Clay, since 1994. As a conference speaker, the author of ten popular books, and a ministry leader, she has helped countless Christian parents build life-giving homes and raise wholehearted children for Christ. As a mother of four, she has inspired thousands of mothers since 1998 through annual Mom Heart Conferences and Mom Heart small groups. Sally encourages many through her blog posts at SallyClarkson.com and MomHeart.com, as well as through her e-books and live webinars. She began her ministry in Communist Eastern Europe with the international ministry CRU and has a passion for discipleship training. Find out more about *Own Your Life* at OwnYourLifeBook.net.

Sally Clarkson

Books and Resources to
Help You Own Your Life

Sally has served Christ in ministry for four decades. She and Clay started Whole Heart Ministries in 1994 to serve Christian parents. Since then, Sally has spoken to thousands of women in her Mom Heart Conferences and written numerous inspirational books about motherhood, faith, and life. She is a regular mom blogger.

ONLINE

SallyClarkson.com – Personal blog for Christian women

MomHeart.com – Ministry blog for Christian mothers

WholeHeart.org – Ministry website, blog, and store

MomHeartConference.com – Ministry conference website

IN PRINT

Seasons of a Mother's Heart (Apologia Press)

The Mission of Motherhood (WaterBrook Press)

The Ministry of Motherhood (WaterBrook Press)

Dancing with My Father (WaterBrook Press)

The Mom Walk (Whole Heart Press)

Desperate (with Sarah Mae, Thomas Nelson)

10 Gifts of Wisdom (Home for Good Books)

You Are Loved (with Angela Perritt, Love God Greatly)

CONTACT INFORMATION

Whole Heart Ministries | Mom Heart Ministry
PO Box 3445 | Monument, CO 80132
719.488.4466 | 888.488.4466 | 888.FAX.2WHM